SAY IT WITH FLOWERS

SAY IT WITH FLOWERS

by Jane Thornton

JOSEF WEINBERGER PLAYS

LONDON

SAY IT WITH FLOWERS
First published in 2010
by Josef Weinberger Ltd
12-14 Mortimer Street, London W1T 3JJ
www.josef-weinberger.com / plays@jwmail.co.uk

Copyright © 2010 by Jane Thornton
Copyright © 2009 by Jane Thornton as an unpublished dramatic composition

The author asserts her moral right to be identified as the author of the work.

ISBN: 978 0 85676 307 6

This play is protected by Copyright. According to Copyright Law, no public performance or reading of a protected play or part of that play may be given without prior authorization from Josef Weinberger Plays, as agent for the Copyright Owners.

From time to time it is necessary to restrict or even withdraw the rights of certain plays. **It is therefore essential to check with us before making a commitment to produce a play. NO PERFORMANCE MAY BE GIVEN WITHOUT A LICENCE**

AMATEUR PRODUCTIONS

Royalties are due at least one calendar month prior to the first performance. A royalty quotation will be issued upon receipt of the following details:

Name of Licensee
Play Title
Place of Performance
Dates and Number of Performances
Audience Capacity and ticket price(s)

PROFESSIONAL PRODUCTIONS

All enquiries regarding professional rights should be addressed to Alan Brodie Representation, Paddock Suite, The Courtyard, 55 Charterhouse Street, London EC1M 6HA.

OVERSEAS PRODUCTIONS

Applications for productions overseas should be made to our local authorised agents. Further information can be found on our website or in our printed Catalogue of Plays.

CONDITIONS OF SALE

This book is sold subject to the condition that it shall not by way of trade or otherwise be re-sold, hired out, circulated or distributed without prior consent of the Publisher. **Reproduction of the text either in whole or part and by any means is strictly forbidden.**

SPECIAL NOTE ON SONGS AND RECORDINGS

Mad Dogs and Englishman lyrics reprinted by kind permission of The Noël Coward Estate. For performance of such songs and recordings mentioned in this play as are in copyright, the permission of the copyright owners must be obtained.

Printed by Commercial Colour Press plc, Hainault, Essex

SAY IT WITH FLOWERS was first presented by Hull Truck Theatre Company (John Godber Creative Director, Gareth Tudor Price Artistic Director) on July 9th 2009 at Hull Truck Theatre, Hull. The cast was as follows:

MAVIS	Annie Sawle
STAN	Dicken Ashworth
VERA	Jacqueline Pilton
RICHARD	James Hornsby
RIO/VICKY	Claire Eden

Directed by John Godber
Designed by Pip Leckenby
Lighting Design by Graham Kirk
Music composed by Stuart Briner

ACT ONE

Scene One

Music.

The patio area at the back of a small bungalow. Twilight, summer. There is a patio table and chairs. On the table is a glass and bottle opener, a small bottle of beer and a packet of crisps. There is a greenhouse off stage and the entrance to STAN'S *shed onstage. The door into the house leads into the kitchen. Either side of the door are hooks for hanging baskets. There is also a gate which leads down the side of the house to the front of the house. Further back beyond the gate and shed we can just see a skylight belonging to* RIO'S *house. On the patio there is a tray filled with seedlings.* STAN, *a man in his sixties enters. He is dressed for gardening and carries a watering can. As he aproaches the stage area we hear the neighbour's dog start barking and throwing himself against the fence.*

STAN   Shut up, you stupid mutt!

            (STAN *goes to fill his watering can from the water butt at the side of the house. The dog keeps barking.*)

            (*to himself*) Bloody nuisance.

            (*He looks at his watch whilst the can is filling, then takes some secateurs from his pocket and snips an infinitesimal amount off the leaves of a nearby plant. He then turns off the water butt, picks up the now full can. The dog whines a bit, then settles down.* STAN *waters the trays of seedlings. He then puts the can back near to the butt, switches the outside lights on, then he starts to stack plant pots into a wheelbarrow. As he is doing this we hear noise come from inside the house as* MAVIS, STAN'S *wife, and her friends* VERA *and* RICHARD *enter. The dog starts up again.*)

STAN   Bloody hell.

MAVIS (*shouting from off*) I'm back!

VERA (*from off*) Where is he?

MAVIS (*from off*) Stanley?

(*The dog keeps barking.*)

STAN Bloody hell!

(MAVIS, VERA and RICHARD (*old friends of hers*) *spill out on to the patio.* MAVIS *is in her late 50s/early 60s. She is lively, flustered and eager to please.* VERA *is more direct and down to earth, not afraid to speak her mind.* RICHARD, *on the other hand, is slightly effeminate and emotional but posesses an acerbic wit.* MAVIS *carries a fancy bottle bag in which there is a bottle of champagne.*)

VERA Well, you've missed a treat.

STAN That's good, then.

VERA It went down bloody smashing, didn't it, Mavis?

STAN I'm just going to shut my greenhouse up.

(STAN *exits with the wheelbarrow.*)

VERA She's so talented, your wife, you know, Stan!

(*The dog quietens down.*)

RICHARD And I know I'm prejudiced, but I think it was our best yet. I mean I loved *My Fair Lady*, don't get me wrong, and *Fiddler* . . .

VERA Oh no, that was chuffin' depressing . . .

RICHARD But tonight it was perfect, I mean I didn't like to say it while we were there, but I thought you did a brilliant job.

MAVIS	Well it's not just me, is it? I mean your set and costumes . . . the whole thing . . .
RICHARD	But a bad director, Mavis, could've ruined it. And the choreography! How you've still got the energy to do it, I don't know! I mean I was a dancer, but I couldn't do it now God help me! My knees wouldn't be up to it. No, honestly!

(*FX: Dog starts barking once more.*)

MAVIS	That dog!
RICHARD	Do you know it's a beautiful garden is this; but that dog's ruining it!
MAVIS	I'm sorry about this . . .

(*FX:* RIO's *voice – dog stops barking.*)

RIO V/O	Gonzo! Shut it and get in here!

(*More hushed tones.*)

VERA	It's since she moved in, isn't it? I mean me and Doug can hear it up t' road, 'bastard thing.
MAVIS	Well you will . . .
VERA	Doug says he'd like to get his hands round its neck.
MAVIS	She never walks it . . .
VERA	Who's got it, Mavis, did you say, the daughter?
MAVIS	That's Rio! The Granddaughter. Can you remember her? She was only knee-high when we last saw her. I mean we looked after Flossie more than they did, and when she dies, Rio moves in! I don't know what the hell she does, Richard, but you should see her.

	Forty years we've been here but these last five weeks: oh hell needy!

(STAN *reappears from the greenhouse.*)

RICHARD	I don't get dogs, they're too needy, they've got to be your best friend. Whereas cats . . .
STAN	I hate bloody cats.
RICHARD	Why's that then, Stan?
STAN	They're allus shitting in my garden.
MAVIS	Do you have to?
STAN	I've just shovelled some up down t' path.
RICHARD	Lovely.
STAN	I dipped one in my water butt other day.
RICHARD	A cat?
STAN	Straight in and out! Not seen it since.
RICHARD	That's awful.
STAN	Didn't kill it, just scared it.
MAVIS	You can get reported for that.
RICHARD	Well don't think you're coming near my cats.
STAN	I don't want to go near anybody's cats.

(STAN *fills up the watering can and wanders off again.*)

MAVIS	They're lovely are Richard's cats.
VERA	What're they called again?
RICHARD	Fred and Ginger.
VERA	Are they ginger then?
MAVIS	It's after Ginger Rogers, Vera . . .

VERA	I know that, Mavis. It's just I thought that one might have been ginger . . .
RICHARD	No they're not, no!
VERA	They're not cat names though are they?
RICHARD	Ginger's a bloody cat's name Vera, what's more a cat's name than that?
VERA	I wouldn't have put it with a Fred though; I mean you're alright shouting 'em in . . .
RICHARD	What about that Champagne, Mavis? I'm in need of a drink.
MAVIS	Ooo sorry. I'll go and open it.
VERA	Cats are called Tiddles or sommat like that.
MAVIS	And you'd go out and shout Tiddles would you?

(MAVIS *exits*.)

VERA	Do you want some help?
RICHARD	Well I wouldn't call a cat of mine Tiddles!

(STAN *comes back, carrying another tray of plants*.)

VERA	What you got there, Stan? Geraniums?
STAN	And some lobelia.
RICHARD	I love lobelia; I mean I know it's common as muck but that deep blue just sets off your Bizzie Lizzies.
VERA	My lobelia's not done so well.
STAN	Probably let it get too dry.

VERA: Well I've been busy painting scenery.

STAN: You can have a bit of that if you want. These are to give to Jim.

VERA: I can swop you for some marigolds.

STAN: No, you're right, Vera, I've got plenty in my cold frames I don't want to put 'em in yet in case there's a frost.

VERA: We'll not get one now, will we?

STAN: You never know with t' weather these days. I mean it's warm tonight and it's only t' beginning of May. But next week it could all change . . .

VERA: I hope it doesn't. I'm wanting to paint my fence.

RICHARD: Have you saved me some Bizzie Lizzies for my baskets?

STAN: And some fuschias, you said. I could have made 'em up.

RICHARD: Oh no, I like to do them myself. I like a theme . . .

STAN: Ar, it's all in is that, themes . . .

RICHARD: I know that.

STAN: They're three pounds a strip are Bizzie Lizzies in t' garden centre and they're not half the size of mine.

RICHARD: Three pounds?

STAN: Not half the size of these.

RICHARD: Well obviously I can pay you if you . . .

STAN: Ah well, a couple of quid wouldn't go amiss.

RICHARD	(*rummages in his pocket and puts two pounds on the table*) No, they look nice them.
STAN	Ar cheers, Richard.
	(MAVIS *re-enters with a tray of glasses and the champagne, now open.*)
MAVIS	Here we go; I mean this is what you came round for and I'm keeping it in my bag! Anyway, help yourselves! Do you want one, Stan?
STAN	No, I'm going to my shed.
MAVIS	Please yourself.
STAN	I will do!
	(STAN *exits to the shed.*)
RICHARD	Come on, we need a toast!
VERA	Course we do!
RICHARD	Can you believe it's been ten years?
MAVIS	Ten years since me and you split from Park Lane Amateurs.
RICHARD	And they *were* amateurs, love.
MAVIS	Oh dear . . . awful!
VERA	That means it's nine years since Doug's been able to get out of the house.
RICHARD	Bless him.
VERA	That's why I got involved; I was sick of being stuck in. Anyway, go on Richard, say a few words.
RICHARD	Well if I must . . . well; where shall I start?

MAVIS: Don't start at the beginning, Richard, we'll be here all night!

RICHARD: Well from *Showboat*, to *The Vagabond King*, from *Rookery Nook* to *Little Shop of Horrors* . . . we've certainly come a long way . . .

MAVIS: And we're still going strong . . . Well, we are when my hip's not playing up.

RICHARD: So raise your glasses to The Parish Players!

(*They raise their glasses.*)

MAVIS: The Parish Players!

VERA: The Parish Players!

RICHARD: To ten amazing years and further success.

(VERA *raises her glass.*)

VERA: To further success!

MAVIS: Because we deserve it.

VERA: Because we work chuffin' hard.

(STAN *appears again.*)

STAN: I'm going to put kettle on.

(*He makes to go.*)

MAVIS: Well we're having a drink, so . . .

VERA: Can I have a cig? I'm bloody desperate.

STAN: As long as you don't leave ash on t' patio.

(STAN *goes into the house.*)

VERA: I'll leave it then.

MAVIS: He's so rude!

VERA: I need to pack it in, but I enjoy it too much.

(*She coughs.*)

MAVIS — He'll be wanting his supper in a minute.

RICHARD — Supper? Who has supper?

VERA — We do, a pot o' tea and a cig, usually . . .

RICHARD — I don't know why you pander to him.

MAVIS — Because it's easier than arguing. I did arguing for thirty-nine years. Why do you think I do my shows?

VERA — I don't pander to Doug. I mean it's not my fault he's agoraphobic. We don't even know what started it. I think it was after his Mam. I look after him, don't get me wrong, but I can't stay in all chuffin' day. He'd like me to but you can only watch *Goldfinger* so many times.

RICHARD — Oh I love *Goldfinger*.

VERA — You can go watch it with him then, Richard.

RICHARD — No, you're all right, Vera.

MAVIS — How much do you think that we'll make for the church fund this year then?

VERA — About another grand, I'd have thought.

MAVIS — They can't complain, can they?

VERA — Oh no!

MAVIS — They probably will, though!

(STAN *comes back out with another beer.*)

STAN — Is there any supper going?

MAVIS — Couldn't you get it yourself?

STAN — I didn't know what there was.

MAVIS	There's some malt bread, do you want some of that?
STAN	Ar, I'll have that and a bit of cheese then. Will you be long?
MAVIS	I'm drinking this first.
STAN	I'll go and watch a bit of football till you come in then.
MAVIS	Fine!
STAN	Only you'll be tired out tomorrow and we've got to do them onion sets, you know. I did tell you!
	(STAN *exits.* MAVIS *whispers to* RICHARD.)
MAVIS	I can't bloody wait.
RICHARD	I can't eat cheese at bed time, gives me terrible dreams.
VERA	It makes me fart.
MAVIS	Oh Vera, too much information!
VERA	In fact it was that bad once it nearly drove Doug outside.
RICHARD	You should eat it more?
MAVIS	Yes that'd cure his agoraphobia!
	(*They laugh.*)
RICHARD	So, what's next? *Sweeney Todd*? *Rent*? *Best Little Whore House* . . .
MAVIS	How about all three?
VERA	She wants to keep busy!
RICHARD	Or the monster!

VERA: What, *Frankenstein*?

RICHARD: *La Cage aux Folles*?

MAVIS: Oh . . . now you're talking . . .

VERA: I can't make pies, not with crepe paper. Anyway we've got to get this year over with yet!

MAVIS: It'll have to be *La Cage Aux Folles* then.

RICHARD: Suits me; I mean the music's fabulous . . . a challenge, but what the hell . . .

(RICHARD *stands*.)

WOHOOO!

(*All three cheer. Their loud antics wake the dog who starts barking from within the house next door.*)

MAVIS: Oh no!

(STAN *comes back out.*)

STAN: I'm just wondering what's happening about this malt bread?

MAVIS: I'm coming, I'm coming.

(MAVIS *goes in with* STAN.)

VERA: He just clicks his fingers.

RICHARD: She's brought it on herself.

VERA: Oh don't.

RICHARD: Why she stays with him is beyond me.

VERA: There must be sommat.

RICHARD: Well I don't get it. But then what do I know about relationships? I've had more than Julio Iglesias. That's why I've got cats.

(RICHARD *helps himself to another drink.*)

VERA I mean I don't know why I chose Doug to be honest. Because he was fat back then and had orange flares, but there must have been a spark!

(*The lights go out on the patio.*)

RICHARD Oh. That's it then, Vera. Looks like it's time to go home.

(*Blackout. Music.*)

Scene Two

The next morning. STAN *enters with a newspaper which he puts down. He then starts clearing glasses, which have been left from the night before, off the table.*

STAN Look at all this! (*Calls.*) You've left these glasses out all night!

(MAVIS *enters in a dressing gown.*)

MAVIS Eh?

STAN I say, you've left these glasses out! They'll be ruined.

MAVIS Why will they?

STAN You should have taken 'em in.

MAVIS Why didn't you take 'em in if you were that bothered?

STAN I was watching t' football.

MAVIS You could have taken 'em in after it finished.

STAN I thought you were going to do it.

MAVIS I was tired, Stan, that's why!

STAN	I don't know why you had to ask 'em round.
	(STAN *inspects is patio.*)
MAVIS	Well they're good friends to me. Not like your mate Jim.
STAN	Jim's alright.
MAVIS	He is! He won't even pay to have his hair cut; he looks like a geriatric Tarzan.
	(*She wipes the table and comes across two pound coins.*)
	Whose is this money?
STAN	It's mine is that.
MAVIS	Well what's it doing out here.?
STAN	Richard gave it me.
MAVIS	What for?
STAN	His Bizzie Lizzies.
MAVIS	You've never charged him?
STAN	It's bloody cheap is that. Have you seen what they are at 'garden centre?
MAVIS	Well not only are you rude . . .
STAN	I wasn't bloody rude.
MAVIS	Now you're charging 'em for a few bloody plants.
STAN	I've got to buy my seed and stuff.
MAVIS	Well you can just give him it back.
STAN	I'm not giving him it back.
MAVIS	I'd rather give you two pounds myself.
STAN	Well you give me two pounds, then.

MAVIS	You've grown too many as it is. You must have five hundred in t' greenhouse. What you going to do with 'em?
STAN	Not give 'em away to Richard!
MAVIS	It's two pounds!
STAN	Two litres of petrol is that.
MAVIS	Good grief.
STAN	You want to get your washing out, it's going to rain later. It's no good leaving it until dinner time like you usually do.
MAVIS	Telling me how to do my washing now.
STAN	If it's out of 'way we can get on with t' onion sets.
MAVIS	Well I might not want to do 'em today,
STAN	I thought you like onions?
MAVIS	I do, but I'll do 'em when I want; not when you tell me.
STAN	Well they need to go in.
MAVIS	Well at least let me have a coffee first.
	(*She exits with glasses, etc.*)
STAN	I'll have a tea if you're putting the kettle on, and is there a bacon sandwich did you say?
	(*Music. Lights.*)

Scene Three

Later. STAN *is slightly more dishevelled, his shirt undone. We catch him closing the shed door. He sits and easily gets comfortable reading the paper. He calls off to* MAVIS.

STAN	Well I'm glad that's done. We've done a good job with them onions.
	(*He looks at the paper, the* Daily Telegraph.)
	I don't know why I read this, it's that depressing. Bloody politicians! I could do better missen.
	(*A beat. He reads once more.*)
	I could save more money, that's for sure. Mind you, it's not difficult. Hot out here!
	(*FX: The dog starts barking.*)
	Oh hell!
RIO	(*shouts, off*) Gonzo . . . shut it!
	(*The dog whimpers into silence*).
STAN	She's up then. Dinner time like, but . . . ! (*To himself.*) Must have dog mess all over t' house, either that or it's got bladder of a donkey.
	(MAVIS *enters, very dishevelled and dirty. She brings out two glasses of orange juice.*)
MAVIS	Look at my nails, and I've got Vicar coming to watch this afternoon.
STAN	There's not a matinee, is there?
MAVIS	You know there is. An OAP matinee.
STAN	On my own again, then?
MAVIS	You're an OAP; you come.
STAN	I'll just get on.
MAVIS	You can hang me that washing out.
STAN	I said to do it this morning.

MAVIS	I've been putting onions in.
STAN	Been a good job, that!
MAVIS	And it's the last time!
STAN	I like an onion.
MAVIS	Why we have to dig seven different kinds of compost in before we start is beyond me! Well I'm not doing it any more, Stanley, I'm getting too old for digging, what with my back!
STAN	Your back's alright when you're dancing.
MAVIS	Well nobody's telling me I'm doing it wrong all the time, are they?
STAN	You won't listen, that's the problem.
MAVIS	I mean I think measuring the distance between each onion with a tape measure is just . . .
STAN	Well you were putting 'em too close together.
MAVIS	It's not like I've not done them before.
STAN	They're different onions this year.

(*A beat.*)

MAVIS	Did our Joanne tell you she was going to Monte Carlo?
STAN	Can you remember when we went? All that way in a Morris Minor?
MAVIS	We must have been daft.
STAN	Ar, we've done some daft stuff.
MAVIS	Isn't it lovely today?

(MAVIS *has a drink, then sits down in a chair to take in the sun.*)

STAN	You'll want some suntan lotion on.
	(MAVIS *ignores him.*)
	Mavis! Don't go to sleep. Mavis?
	(*A beat.*)
	You need some suntan lotion on.
MAVIS	Can't you just sit quiet?
STAN	I'm only saying.
MAVIS	Have you got suntan lotion on?
STAN	I don't burn like you.
MAVIS	I'm only going to be twenty minutes then I'm going to get a shower.
STAN	It was thirty five degrees in t' greenhouse, and that was this morning.
MAVIS	Well I'm not sat in the greenhouse, am I?
STAN	Well you're daft not putting sommat on.
MAVIS	Well I'm daft then!
STAN	Bloody burn then!
MAVIS	I will do.
STAN	Oh I'm going to my shed.
	(*He turns and makes to go as* VERA *enters through the house.*)
VERA	Did you know your door was open?
STAN	That's you, that!
MAVIS	It would be!
VERA	I've just rung church hall to book for next year; I thought I'd get on with it . . .

MAVIS	Oh hell, Vera . . . keen!
VERA	But it turns out they don't want us.
MAVIS	Eh?
VERA	That new dance school they have in on Thursdays, Miss Feather's or whatever it's called, is going to be doing a show.
MAVIS	Well I don't see why they can't they have both?
VERA	Well apparently t' bowling club wants a lot more nights, so they've no spare rehearsal time.
MAVIS	No spare what?
VERA	They've just dumped us.
MAVIS	Just like that? After all we've done?
VERA	This is what she's just told me!
MAVIS	And all money we've raised for 'em?
VERA	Bastards!
MAVIS	Exactly!
VERA	They were going to tell us at t' end of the week, she said!
MAVIS	I can't believe it.
VERA	I mean I daren't tell Richard.
STAN	I've said to you before! You do it all for nowt and truth is they don't give that about you. Never mind petrol money it's cost over t' years.
MAVIS	Oh shut up, you.
STAN	You know I'm right though, that's what hurts!
VERA	Why don't you go and put kettle on, Stan?

STAN	Who me?
VERA	You just fill it with water and press t' switch.
STAN	We've got a bloody comedian here now.
MAVIS	He'll get that wrong, Vera.
STAN	Do you want sugar?
VERA	Just one for me.
STAN	They've used you, I said all along that they would.
	(STAN *exits*.)
MAVIS	It's just bloody unbelievable!
VERA	What, Stan putting t' kettle on?
MAVIS	That and all!
VERA	It's like Doug says; why have they suddenly changed their minds?
MAVIS	I'll tell you why; it's her, Miss Feather.
VERA	How come?
MAVIS	Vicky Feather; runs the dance school, she's a right pushy madam! And I'll tell you what; she's never liked us as a family. She was in our Joanne's class at school.
VERA	That's going back.
MAVIS	She went home crying because our Joanne got Snow White in t' Christmas pantomime and she was stuck with a dwarf.
VERA	Which dwarf was it, do you know?
MAVIS	I can't remember, Vera!
VERA	Because I was Dopey at school.

MAVIS   I bet you was!

VERA   In the bloody play, you . . .

MAVIS   She was rubbish and all, couldn't sing but she thought she was Julie Andrews. Still does!

VERA   I think I was Dopey, but it might've been Doc. I'll have to ask Doug.

MAVIS   Vicky Feather's doing a bloody show now?

VERA   No, I was Dopey! Yes I was! I thought I was!

MAVIS   So, what are we going to do?

VERA   Doug says we should keep this year's money. Go on a cruise or . . .

MAVIS   We can't do that. Can we?

VERA   Course we can.

MAVIS   I don't fancy a cruise, though. I don't like boats.

VERA   Stan does, he loves 'em, doesn't he?

MAVIS   Canal boats, and he wouldn't be coming anyway!

VERA   We could use it to start again . . .

MAVIS   Again?

VERA   Somewhere new!

MAVIS   Maybe we should call it a day?

(STAN *appears from inside the house.*)

STAN   There's Rio here from next door, lost her rabbit or sommat.

MAVIS   Her rabbit?

STAN	Hey, don't shoot the messenger!
MAVIS	Oh tell her to come back later, will you? . . .
STAN	Well she seems a bit upset, so . . .
MAVIS	Well I don't want it at moment, Stan . . .
VERA	What's happened to t' cup of tea?

(RIO *appears. She is a large-framed, softly-spoken Goth.*)

RIO	Alright then, Mrs Clayton?
MAVIS	Hello, Rio!
VERA	Rio?
RIO	I've lost my rabbit.
MAVIS	Well that's not good, is it?
STAN	What colour is it, then?

(RIO *looks around the garden.*)

RIO	What?
STAN	Your rabbit?
RIO	Grey! Sort of grey. Made a nice job, haven't you? A pond and all?
STAN	Well I've not seen it, unless it's got between shed and t' greenhouse.
RIO	Got out of its cage.
VERA	Maybe your dog's had it?
MAVIS	Aye, it's quiet today, Rio.
RIO	I've put a muzzle on it. It's a nuisance really.
STAN	Well I can't argue with that.

RIO	It's not even mine, it's my mate's. She's gone backpacking in Thailand.
MAVIS	And when's she back, then?
RIO	A couple of years, I think.
MAVIS	That's good then!
RIO	She's finding herself.
MAVIS	She ought to come back and find her bloody dog!
STAN	She might come back and find it strung up, one day!
RIO	I wish I could find my rabbit, though.
	(*Pointing to a tray of plants.*)
	Are they geraniums?
STAN	They are, yes!
RIO	I thought they were. My dad used to grow them. When we lived in the caravan. He used to put 'em all round outside, then spend all day watering 'em. Mind you, he'd nowt else to do.
MAVIS	Sounds like somebody I know!
RIO	Can I have some for my garden?
STAN	You what?
RIO	Can I have some of them Geraniums?
STAN	Well I don't really give 'em away, you see . . .
RIO	You've got loads though haven't you? If I got some flowers I'd tidy my garden up!
MAVIS	He'll let you have 'em for a couple of quid Rio. I mean that's nearly two litres, isn't it Stan?

Rio	Oh, I can't afford to pay for 'em.
Stan	Well I'll see if I can pot you some up.
Rio	Don't give me all 'crap 'uns.
Stan	There aren't any crap ones when I grow 'em, are they, Vera?
Vera	No, they're all good plants are Stan's.
Rio	Anyway if you catch my rabbit, chuck it back over, will you?
Vera	You want to watch it with Stan; it might end up in his water barrel.
Mavis	Don't worry, if we catch it we'll bring it round.
Rio	I like them pots. Where are they from then, B & Q?
Mavis	Our daughter brought 'em from Italy.
Rio	Oh, I've been to Florence.
Mavis	Have you?
Rio	Years ago, with school.
Mavis	We have, when we went to visit.
Stan	That was in the days when we could afford it. We've not much chance of going there now.
Mavis	Oh . . . Mr Sunshine . . .
Stan	You didn't like it anyway.
Mavis	I didn't like plane, I liked Florence. I'd go back to there.
Rio	Bit old though, isn't it?

VERA	I've never been to Italy. I hate pizzas anyway, so . . .
	(FX: *The dog barks once more.*)
RIO	I don't believe it.
MAVIS	No, I don't!
RIO	He must have chewed through his muzzle now.
	(*Shouts to dog.*)
	Shut up you stupid sod! Friggin' hell!
	(RIO *starts to exit.*)
VERA	You could allus kill it, Rio, if it's not yours!
	(RIO *stares at her coldly.*)
RIO	I'll come back for my plants later.
STAN	I'll sort you a few out, then!
RIO	Don't forget about my rabbit, will you?
MAVIS	How could we?
RIO	Gonzo! Shut it! Gonzo!
	(RIO *exits.*)
MAVIS	Gonzo! Rio! Sometimes I wonder where we're living!
STAN	It's a funny style that, isn't it?
MAVIS	It's Goth, isn't it?
RIO	(*off*) Shut it.
STAN	I'll go look for this rabbit then!
	(STAN *exits down the side of the shed.*)

VERA	Yes, my niece brought one round at Christmas. Doug shat hissen; he thought grim reaper had turned up.
MAVIS	I was just thinking; you know that this Vicky Feather is the Lady Mayor, don't you? Her husband's Frank Feather. He's a lot older than her!
VERA	I know who you mean; he's a property developer. That's why she's t' Lady Mayor!
MAVIS	Mind you, she's still stuck with a bloody dwarf, isn't she?
VERA	Is she?
MAVIS	Well Frank Feather's tiny, isn't he? He came to see *The Student Prince* and we had to put him on a box!
VERA	Who'd've thought they'd do it to you, Mavis? The stinking . . .
MAVIS	Don't say it, Vera, just think it!
VERA	I am thinking it!

(*A beat.*)

The stinking lousy bastards!

(*Music. Lights*)

Scene Four

The patio; Sunday morning after The Parish Players' last night. RICHARD *enters with a small bunch of half-dead flowers which he attempts to arrange in a vase. He has placed some Ferrero Rocher chocolates on the table.*

RICHARD	It's outrageous, absolutely outrageous. I mean look at them; I wouldn't make them into

	compost. Ten years and over ten thousand pounds we've given to the Church Hall and look at what they've the cheek to give us. A bunch of dead Chrysants and some Ferrero Rocher. Honestly, I don't know how they dare. I know they reckon you can "Say it with Flowers"; well they've certainly made the message clear with this sorry lot.

(MAVIS *has entered in her dressing gown.*)

MAVIS   Don't let it get to you, Richard.

RICHARD   I can't help it. It's unforgivable.

MAVIS   There's nowt we can do.

RICHARD   You can't pretend it doesn't hurt.

MAVIS   When did they give you 'em, anyway?

RICHARD   As I was leaving. They were looking for you, but you'd gone.

MAVIS   I didn't want to hang around.

RICHARD   They should have presented them to us on stage, that's what they should have done. Mind you, looking at them it would have been embarrassing, wouldn't it?

MAVIS   They can shove them up their arse for all I'm bothered.

RICHARD   Oooh, don't let the bastards grind you down. And I'll tell you something: what a night. What a fantastic one to go out on. I mean they absolutely gave it their all, didn't they? And we'll find somewhere else, you know.

MAVIS   Well I don't know whether I've the heart for it any more. It's all geared to young people, isn't it, these days? That's what 'Vicar said, it's so we can give young people a chance. I don't know what chance they give us.

RICHARD	None, but we can't let that stop us.
	(RICHARD *spots the time*.)
	Oh hells bells! Where's this morning gone? I've got to go I've got my aqua class and if I miss it I'm stiff as a board.
MAVIS	Well thanks for bringing 'em.
RICHARD	The thing is if I'd left them any longer they would have been dead.
MAVIS	I'll do something with them.
RICHARD	Yes, bin them. I'll pop in later in the week. We need a plan.
MAVIS	I'll save you a chocolate.
RICHARD	I can't wait!
	(STAN *enters, carrying a paper*.)
RICHARD	Been for your paper?
STAN	Bit early for you, isn't it, Richard?
RICHARD	Oh no, not on Sundays; I'm up and about. Tara!
MAVIS	Tara!
	(*A beat*.)
STAN	What's he doing here?
MAVIS	He brought these flowers, they're from t' Church Hall committee.
STAN	Are they a joke?
MAVIS	I don't think so, no.
STAN	Bloody hell, pathetic.
MAVIS	That's what Richard said.

STAN   He's here a lot at moment, isn't he?

MAVIS   Not really.

STAN   Has he gone up to Vera's an' all?

MAVIS   I don't know, why?

STAN   Well what you doing in your dressing gown?

MAVIS   I've just got up.

STAN   Oh right!

MAVIS   What are you trying to say?

STAN   You being like that when he's here.

MAVIS   It's only Richard.

STAN   Ar, I know.

MAVIS   What's up with you?

STAN   Well it's not rate, is it?

MAVIS   What do you mean?

STAN   It's too familiar.

MAVIS   Give over, me and Richard's shared a dressing room and everything. We've been friends for years.

STAN   He's never away at moment!

MAVIS   We've been doing a show. Neither is Vera; shall I change out of my dressing gown if she comes around as well?

STAN   You spend more time with him than me.

MAVIS   Oh!

STAN   Well I'm beginning to wonder.

MAVIS   For God's . . . Richard's not interested in me.

STAN	How do you know?
MAVIS	Because it's not his thing is it?
STAN	What isn't?
MAVIS	Women! You've never just realised? I thought you were slow, but . . .
STAN	Well I thought there was sommat, obviously . . .
MAVIS	He has . . . friends. He goes to clubs.
STAN	What clubs?
MAVIS	Special clubs, how do I know?
STAN	What? Round here?
MAVIS	How do I know?
STAN	Well I'm not so keen on that!
MAVIS	Well he's not asking you to go with him, is he?
STAN	I should think he's bloody not.
MAVIS	It's none of our business. Richard's my friend, he's kind, and he makes me laugh, that's all I'm bothered about.
STAN	You've allus been t'same. Hanging about with t' likes of Richard and Vera! In fact she's more of a bloke than him.
MAVIS	What? I mean, where's all this coming from?
STAN	From me, because I think that it's gone on long enough.
MAVIS	Oh do you?
STAN	And now you've a chance now to leave it and spend a bit more time at home.
MAVIS	So that's what this is all about.

STAN	Well I think you need to!
MAVIS	What, and end up digging for you?
STAN	Well if you're gonna be stupid about it.
MAVIS	Because that's what you'd like! Me to pack everything in and be at your beck and call.
STAN	Well we could do more together.
MAVIS	Well I wanted us to go to Italian classes but you wouldn't even give it a look.
STAN	What do I want to learn Italian for at my age?
MAVIS	I don't know; seeing as we aren't ever going to be going back to Italy . . .
STAN	Well, with t' interest rates . . .
MAVIS	And when are we going to see our Joanne?
STAN	She's making plenty of money, she can always come here.
MAVIS	We've a lot more spare time.
STAN	Well she if wants to see us, she can pay for us to fly over. I mean, she chose to live in Italy!
MAVIS	It was a brilliant opportunity for her, you know it was.
STAN	She didn't give a shit about us, though.
MAVIS	I didn't expect her to! Oh you're such a funny bugger.
STAN	What, and you're not?
MAVIS	I'm not as funny as you!

(STAN *makes to exit.*)

STAN	Anyway, I'm going to do my boat.
MAVIS	That's what you'll be wanting me to join next; the model boat club!
STAN	I don't, I go to that with Jim!
MAVIS	Thank God.
STAN	Well I've oft' thought we might clean the caravan up and go off somewhere but . . .
MAVIS	You thought I'd clean it up you mean, 'cos that's what usually happens. We haven't been in it for years.
STAN	Well we'd do it in no time!
MAVIS	And where would we go? Wales? The Lake District? Cleethorpes? Grange over Sands? Wow. Hang on, I'll go and clean it up now!
STAN	Oh, forget it, I'm going to get on! Wear what the bloody hell you like!

(STAN *exits.* MAVIS *is frustrated in many ways.*)

(*Lights. Music.*)

Scene Five

Two weeks later. The patio: RIO *is on stage alone. She looks around the patio, touches various flowers and pots. She looks long and hard at the little pond.* VERA *enters from the house.*

VERA	Don't jump!
RIO	Did he do all this?
VERA	Oh aye, Stan, he can make owt. Used to do all the sets in the early days. But then he lost interest.
RIO	Sex?

VERA	Sets? Theatre sets, for the Parish Players. Your Grandma used to come a lot. Oh aye, he did some smashing stuff did Stan.
	(RIO *and* VERA *wander on the patio.*)
RIO	What's he doing now did you say?
VERA	He's gone to get your rabbit; made it a special box.
RIO	What for?
VERA	So you can carry it about.
RIO	I'm only taking it home, not friggin shopping!
VERA	For God's sake, humour him. He's made it for you specially.
	(STAN *enters with a wooden box with the rabbit in it.*)
STAN	Here we are!
RIO	Oh, right then.
STAN	Only you wasn't in and it was eating through the cardboard box I'd put it in, so . . .
RIO	Oh, right then.
STAN	I had some spare wood so . . . It's better off in this.
RIO	It's good that, isn't it?
STAN	There's holes in for it to breathe, and you can let this end down for it to run out and into t' cage.
RIO	You should go on *Dragon's Den* with that.
STAN	It was Vera that spotted it. By God it can move.

Rio	I know that, I've been trying to catch it for two weeks!
Vera	I told Doug, I thought it was a rat at first; frightened me to death.
Rio	Have you got *my* plants and all?
Stan	Ar now, I'm glad you've asked because I'm not sure that I've got any spare. I've a few more baskets than I thought.
Rio	Well I've gone and bought some pots, that's all!
Vera	He'll have a few spare, won't you Stan?
Stan	Well . . .
Rio	Oh it doesn't matter, if you don't want me to have any.
Stan	No, it's not that.
Rio	I mean you said I could so I went out to B & Q . . . I mean if you've changed your tune, fair enough! And I'll bring this box back later.
Stan	No, no this is what I'm saying you can keep that.
Rio	No, I'll bring it back. I don't want to take owt you don't want me to have!
	(Rio *exits with the box.* Vera *and* Stan *take a moment to look at each other.*)
Vera	You've got a few plants spare, haven't you?
Stan	I've got plenty, Vera, but they'll not get looked after, will they?
Vera	How do you know?
Stan	Because she's struggling with a dog and a rabbit. They'd be dead overnight.

VERA	But you'd be building bridges, wouldn't you?
STAN	Well hang on lass, I've made her a box and she dun't bloody want it. Did you want Mavis?
VERA	Well aye, if she's . . .
STAN	Probably still in bed . . .
VERA	Is she alright?
STAN	A fortnight she's been like this. Since that show finished all she's done is sleep.
VERA	Well Doug's been off it, that's why I've not been down much. He's got a rate cold on his chest.

(MAVIS *appears in an old tracksuit.*)

STAN	You've managed to get up, then.
MAVIS	I'll stay in bed all day if I want. I'm retired, aren't I? When you're retired you're supposed to be able to please yourself, aren't you, Vera?
VERA	Oh aye, it's rate is that!
STAN	I thought you were going to do us some meat pies.
MAVIS	Are you wanting me, Vera?
VERA	Just I came for a chat.
STAN	Don't be getting chatting because if you start making them pies much later there'll not be ready for dinner and t' oven won't be on off-peak any more.
MAVIS	Telling me how to make a meat pie now; and I've not got washing out, so that's another thing.

STAN	Oh I can't talk to her. I've got my rudder on my boat; do you want to come and have a look Vera?
VERA	Well . . .
MAVIS	No she doesn't, she's come to see me, not your boat.
STAN	Oh well, I know when I'm not wanted.
MAVIS	Why don't you finish it and then we'll look at it. He's been making it three bloody years.
STAN	I've not been doing it that long.
MAVIS	Well that's what it seems like.
STAN	Let me know when dinner's ready. I'm going to do a bit of weeding at 'front.

(STAN *exits*.)

VERA	Aww, don't be so bloody awful to him, poor sod.
MAVIS	He's awful to me.
VERA	What's up with you?
MAVIS	I'm fed up, that's what's up with me!
VERA	You'd be fed up if you lived with Doug; he's just discovered Bid TV.
MAVIS	Bid TV?
VERA	This morning three pairs of Scholls, a Japanese duvet set and some craft scissors arrived and we're still waiting for a mock-leather coat and a set of suitcases. Which'll be useful, seeing as we're never likely to go anywhere.
MAVIS	You might go on your own.

VERA	Well if I do I'll not need five.
MAVIS	No, five suitcases is a lot!
VERA	And he's gone mad this morning 'cos I've hidden 'credit card.
MAVIS	It's sommat for him to do though, isn't it?
VERA	Way he's going he'll have us bankrupt by next Friday.
MAVIS	Well there is that.
VERA	I mean I can't believe Doug; he's fat as a pig and full of cold but he passed on set of vitamins and a bloody exercise bike. Why didn't he buy them?

(*A beat.*)

Have you not seen Richard?

MAVIS	Well you know what he's like. I think he's got trouble at work, but he never says. I think the shop's under threat, to be honest.
VERA	Well there's not much call for gent's outfitters these days, is there? I mean, saw a suit in Sainsburys t' other day for twenty quid.
MAVIS	And you can't beat that, can you? Not even on Bid TV.

(*A beat.*)

VERA	No. I thought I'd come down and we could decide what we're gonna do next.
MAVIS	Ophh! I don't know!
VERA	I thought we could move to Methodist Hall; I mean there isn't a bar but . . . But we've got to do sommat, haven't we?

MAVIS	I haven't, I've to stay at home according to Stan.
VERA	Oh, take no bloody notice.
MAVIS	He wants me to spend more time with him.
VERA	Or what?
MAVIS	Or my life will be not worth living.
VERA	It'll not be worth living if you're stuck at home all t' time.
MAVIS	I'll not be stuck at home, he's thinking of getting the caravan going again.
VERA	Oh Jesus!
MAVIS	Oph!
VERA	You'll go chuffin' mad.
MAVIS	I know that.
VERA	I mean I'm not being funny, but he's a miserable sod is Stan.
MAVIS	(*shaking her head*) Pppphhh!
VERA	And you can't tell him owt.
MAVIS	Oph that!
VERA	I mean he dun't believe that Doug's poorly.
MAVIS	I know!
VERA	He told me that there's no such a thing as agoraphobia, he thinks Doug's just a lazy twat.
MAVIS	I know; he told me!
VERA	I mean it's difficult with Doug, you know?
MAVIS	I know.

VERA	I mean we both need sommat to do.
MAVIS	Well I'm fed up with arguing, I'm fed up of everything I do being wrong.

(*A beat.*)

VERA	Well why do you stop with him?
MAVIS	We had some great times when we were young, and with our Joanne. I don't know when it changed.
VERA	You have all them years giving to every bugger else, your husband, your kids, then your Mam and Dad need looking after and suddenly you wake up and think, bugger me! I've done nowt and I'm nearly dead!
MAVIS	Oh hell, Vera.
VERA	That's when you want to change things and folks don't like it. Because you're not doing what they want. And I wouldn't say this to anybody else, but Doug first got poorly when I started doing Tai Chi.
MAVIS	Give over?
VERA	I know it might be a coincidence but . . .
VERA	But I'll tell you something; don't think if you stop everything you'll be back to a bed of roses, because it's too late; once they become grumpy old sods you're stuck with 'em.
MAVIS	Oh hell, Vera!
VERA	So you might as well keep doing sommat you like.

(MAVIS *becomes tearful.*)

MAVIS	I don't know. He gets nasty. He says all sorts. I mean he's told me we can't go and see our Joanne because it's too expensive. And going

	to Italy and doing t' show was what I looked forward to.
	(STAN *with the post and a box of weeds.*)
STAN	You're sat out here and it's freezing.
VERA	We're coming in for a drink in a minute.
STAN	Gonna rain, I think it said. Here there's post. More bloody bills and a load of junk mail. The paper they waste! It's a disgrace.
	(*He puts the post down on the table next to* VERA. STAN *holds a local leaflet flyer.*)
	And look at this: "Village in Bloom" competition? They've got that bloody woman on t' back again, showing her baskets off. They're all foliage; there's no bloody flowers in 'em to call owt. Village in Bloom? They don't know what they're talking about!
MAVIS	No, they wouldn't do.
STAN	Anyhow I'm taking these to 'compost. If you're making a drink, I'll have a cuppa tea.
	(STAN *exits.* MAVIS *looks at the leaflet he has left open on the table and studies it.*)
MAVIS	Hey he's right, you know. There's not many flowers on these – look!
VERA	Village in bloody Bloom; who the hell would want to enter some thing like that?
MAVIS	I'll tell you who, Vera; a load of bloody saddos with nowt better to do.
VERA	Exactly!
	(*Lights. Music.*)

Scene Six

RICHARD *sits reading a brochure for the "Village in Bloom" competition.* VERA *pushes on a wheelbarrow full of pots.*

RICHARD	So which section are we going to enter? "Containers and Hanging Baskets"? Or "Urban Garden"?
VERA	We've got to stick to continers and hanging baskets and not spread ussen's too thin.
RICHARD	I wish I could spread myself thin, I've put on at least three pounds this week.
VERA	You can't tell.
RICHARD	Oh pull the other one, Vera, I bet you say that to all the boys! I bet Doug's butter in your hands!
VERA	Chance would be a fine thing.
RICHARD	Yes! I know what you mean!
	(VERA *places the barrow down.*)
VERA	Where's Mavis? We need to choose these pots.
RICHARD	Gone to talk to Stan. He's doing his boat.
	(*FX: The dog starts barking.*)
VERA	Oh, here we go . . .
RICHARD	Well that'll have to stop on judging day, won't it? I mean we won't stand a chance if somebody doesn't shoot that pissing dog!
VERA	She reckons she's had it muzzled.
RICHARD	What's she like, then?
VERA	Well let's just say that she's scarier than the dog! She's one of them Goths.

RICHARD	Oph!
VERA	She's doing tourism at college, Mavis said; customer bloody service. Well I wouldn't want her serving me. She looks like one of the living dead. Stan made her a box, you know.
RICHARD	Not to sleep in?
VERA	No, for her rabbit.
RICHARD	Oh hell Vera, now you've lost me!

(*We hear* RIO'S *voice coming from over the fence.*)

RIO	(*off*) Will you friggin' shut it? Gonzo, shut it! Come here! Come here, will you? Stay . . . come here . . . stay. Stay put!
RICHARD	Not much customer service there, then?
RIO	(*off*) Stay! Sit!
RICHARD	Mind you, she could always work at Little Chef.
RIO	(*off*) Stay! Stay!

(*The dog whimpers in silence.*)

VERA	Looks like t' muzzle's back on.
RICHARD	Or she's strangled it.
RIO	Now get in! Go on, get!

(RIO *and Gonzo 'exit' as a door closes. We hear the sound of an argument coming from inside the shed.*)

STAN	(*off*) You're not listening to me, are you?
RICHARD	Oh, Monty Don's off!
VERA	I like him!
RICHARD	Don't we all!

MAVIS	(*off*) Well stick 'em up your arse, Stanley!
RICHARD	Oh dear!
MAVIS	(*off*) I'll go get some from B & Q!
RICHARD	It's not going well in there.
STAN	(*off*) Let every bugger hear you.
MAVIS	(*off*) You're like a big kid!
STAN	(*off*) I don't want to get involved, that's all I'm saying.

(MAVIS *enters, followed by* STAN. VERA *and* RICHARD *try to pretend they haven't heard the argument.*)

MAVIS	Have you heard this?
RICHARD	Most of it!
MAVIS	We can't have any of his flowers.
VERA	Oh, Stan!
MAVIS	He's only grown five thousand but apparently he needs 'em for himself. I don't know why because they grow and then they die, but . . .
STAN	You can have a few, I said.
MAVIS	Two bloody boxes!
VERA	Well I've got some Bizzie Lizzies spare, so . . .
MAVIS	That's not the point, Vera!
STAN	I'm saving some for Jim . . .
MAVIS	Jim's got to have some, Vera, because he's always helping us out is Jim. He's round here all the bloody time with his Tarzan locks.
STAN	Anyway my hanging baskets aren't done yet.

VERA	But aren't we going to use your hanging baskets as part of the display?
MAVIS	No, we can't because Stan doesn't want to be involved.
RICHARD	Oh, Stanley . . . where's your competitive edge?
MAVIS	He complains that I'm leaving him out and when I ask him to join in he says he doesn't want to be invovled.
STAN	It's just not my thing.
MAVIS	Well if you're not interested in plants what are you bloody interested in?
VERA	Boats, aren't you?
STAN	I *am* interested in plants, I'm not interested in bloody competitions. I never have been; they're for farts.
RICHARD	So now we know!
STAN	It's same folk that wins year after year, it's all sewn up.
MAVIS	All the more reason to change things!
STAN	Half of t' plants are bought from bloody nurseries! They've been kept in greenhouses to bring 'em on.
VERA	Well yours are in t' green house, aren't they?
STAN	Not all of 'em, there isn't room!
MAVIS	Well, can't we buy another greenhouse?
STAN	And where we gonna put it? In t' middle of t' patio?
MAVIS	Why can't you just help us?

STAN	They're not proper gardeners, them people that do them competitions.
VERA	What are they, then?
MAVIS	Bloody Martians, according to him!
STAN	They buy stuff from professionals, slap it in a container and make it look nice. They don't take it seriously.
RICHARD	Well I beg to differ, I don't think that's actually true. I think people take it very seriously.
MAVIS	Hey, don't forget; Stan knows everything, Richard.
RICHARD	Oh yes, I forgot!
STAN	Hey would they know how to grow a cucumber or some tomatoes?
VERA	They don't need to grow cucumbers and tomatoes, do they?
MAVIS	Oh don't, Vera; leave him.
VERA	I mean, I might be wrong but they're not going to look good in patio pots, are they?
STAN	Well cherry tomatoes do.
MAVIS	You'll not win, Vera, whatever you say. (*To* STAN.) Forget it, I wish I'd never asked you. It sounds like if they've not been in a greenhouse they'll not be good enough anyway, so we'll buy some from a nursery. If you can't beat 'em join 'em! We'll show you, we're going to do some brilliant displays, aren't we, Vera?
VERA	If you say so!
MAVIS	Aren't we, Richard?

RICHARD	Absolutely!
	(MAVIS *turns to exit the house.*)
MAVIS	Right, anyone want a cuppa before we start?
RICHARD	I'll have one; all this excitement's made me parched!
STAN	Well I'm going to finish my compost heap.
MAVIS	Well why don't you stick yourself on it while you're there?
	(MAVIS *exits; she is becoming quite upset.*)
VERA	You've done it now, Stan.
RICHARD	I'm saying nothing.
STAN	That'll make a change!
RICHARD	Excuse me?
VERA	Leave it, Richard.
RICHARD	I'm not being spoken to like that.
STAN	Bugger off then, it's my house. I can say what I want.
RICHARD	Well I just might.
STAN	Please yoursen; gate's there!
VERA	Hey now, come on . . .
RICHARD	Do you think it suits you being spiteful, Stan?
STAN	I'm not wrong all the bloody time.
VERA	No you're not, Stan, fair enough, now leave it Richard, will you?
RICHARD	No, I wont!
STAN	Well I've never said owt, but . . .

VERA Let's leave it!

RICHARD Well I'm not putting up with this. In fact I'll tell Mavis that I don't think I'm going to be able to be involved.

VERA Oh shut up, you bloody fart! He dun't mean owt. He's being a silly bugger, that's all.

STAN I'm not.

VERA 'Course you are.

RICHARD It's not acceptable, Vera.

VERA Come on, Stan, what's up with you? You've known Richard for bloody years.

STAN Well I don't want Mavis doing this every minute of every day through t' summer. It's not bloody fair. It got like that with her bloody concerts.

RICHARD Well I wonder why, Stanley; have you ever thought about that?

STAN Why should I be on my own all t' bloody time? While she's fannying about?

RICHARD We're not fannying about?

STAN How would you know?

VERA Hey, Stan, now listen . . .

STAN And now my garden's being taken over.

VERA We'll make 'em up in no time then it's just a bit of watering and that.

STAN It'll take more time than you think.

VERA Listen, if you don't want to be part of it, we'll do it on us own. We'll get us own plants, and we'll do us own thing and nobody's gonna

	bother you! You can just get on with your tomatoes and cucumbers and everything'll be as right as rain. Won't it, Richard?
RICHARD	Don't ask me, I'm not going to be involved.
VERA	For chuff's sake!
RICHARD	Well I'm not!
VERA	I'll tell you sommat: you don't know you're born, you two. At least you've got a bloody choice. Doug's stuck at home by hissen.
STAN	Yeh, but you could get him pricking stuff out for you, couldn't you?
VERA	Well he might have to now, because I've put application form in, haven't I?
RICHARD	You've what?
VERA	I've put the application form in.
RICHARD	When?
VERA	Well you've got to, or all t' places go.
STAN	You're gonna have to get some plug plants now, then.
RICHARD	Plug plants? What the bloody hell are plug plants?
STAN	'Cos there'll be nowt ready if you grow from seed. You haven't time!

(STAN *exits down the garden.*)

VERA	Bloody plug plants now! Where are we gonna get them from?
STAN	Don't bloody ask me; I know nowt about gardening. I'm going in here.

(STAN *exits into his shed.*)

VERA   Bloody hell, Richard! Men? What are you like?

RICHARD   Well don't blame me!

             (*Lights. Music.*)

                    Scene Seven

A few weeks later. Enter MAVIS, *clearly flustered, through the side gate. She pulls a small trolley which contains large pots of Italian origin. She delivers the trolley on stage, huffs and puffs, and then exits inside the house. Moments later,* RIO *appears from near the shed and looks at the pots.* MAVIS *enters carrying a tray full of glasses and a jug of Pimm's with fruit in it. They have been half-used.*

MAVIS   What are you doing, Rio?

RIO   Nowt!

MAVIS   What do you want?

RIO   Can I borrow some pegs?

MAVIS   You can't just come into our garden.

MAVIS   What were you doing down there?

RIO   Just having a look.

MAVIS   You've no business.

RIO   I need some pegs!

MAVIS   Well . . .

RIO   I haven't got enough to hang my stuff out.

MAVIS   Well I don't think I've any spare.

RIO   Well have a look, will you? Otherwise I'll have to go next door! And he's creepy.

MAVIS   Eh?

Rio	Can you have a look?
Mavis	No, I can't!
Rio	I know you don't like me.
Mavis	Well there's little wonder, is there, when I find you wandering round my garden.
Rio	I thought it was his garden?
Mavis	It's *our* garden!
Rio	I thought you did them shows at the Church Hall?
Mavis	Not any more.
Rio	Well I only came for some pegs; thought you might have dropped some, just looking!
Mavis	Well I'm a bit busy right now, so . . .
Rio	Your arse twitches every time you talk to me.
Mavis	Well I don't know how you work that out!
Rio	And he wouldn't give me any plants.
Mavis	His name's Stanley.
Rio	I know what he's called; my Gran used to tell me about him.
Mavis	Did she?
Rio	Wouldn't spend a penny if a halfpenny would do, she said.
Mavis	Your Gran was poorly for a long time, wasn't she?
Rio	Still had it all up here though! (*Touches her head.*)

MAVIS	I'm sure she did.
RIO	He could have easily spared some; there's loads down there. If you needed sommat from me . . .

(MAVIS *takes the pegs of the hook by the door and gives them to* RIO.)

MAVIS	Here, take what you want; make sure you bring them back, that's all.
RIO	You think I'm gonna nick 'em?
MAVIS	No, look . . . I'm busy, so . . .
RIO	You been having a drink, then?
MAVIS	Eh? Well!
RIO	In the middle of the afternoon an' all!
MAVIS	Well.
RIO	Aye, my Gran said you often had drinks and that, in the daytime Like she said; don't know who you think you are? Doing shows, and stuff. Drinking on the patio, doing sommat you shouldn't!
MAVIS	Well, anyway . . .

(VERA *and* RICHARD *arrive, huffing and puffing as they struggle through the gates with two hanging baskets each.* VERA *still holds a basket.*)

VERA	Is everything alright?
MAVIS	Yes, yes. Rio was just going. Popped round for some pegs.
RIO	(*to* RICHARD) You looking at?
RICHARD	Your tights.

RIO	Eh?
RICHARD	I think they're very . . . well . . .
	(*A beat.*)
RIO	I'll go and see if t' dog wants a piss.
	(RIO *exits.* RICHARD *starts to stick labels on the baskets and pots.*)
VERA	What's going on?
MAVIS	She was in t' garden when I got back.
VERA	You want to watch her.
MAVIS	She gives me the creeps, to be honest. I mean you read things, don't you!
VERA	You want to get a lock on that gate.
RICHARD	So what time is Mr Happy back then, Mavis?
MAVIS	Model boat show finishes at four; then they've to drive back. So I can play out for a bit longer, Richard.
RICHARD	That's good, then.
MAVIS	Have you brought all the plants down now, then?
VERA	There's a couple of pots still on t' drive. Can we put these up on them hooks?
MAVIS	(VERA *moves towards a hook on the house.*) Oh I don't know; they're for Stan's little tomatoes.
VERA	Eh?
MAVIS	Oh aye, Vera, he's got a hook for every plant!
RICHARD	Oh dear, anal or what?
MAVIS	You said it, Richard!

RICHARD	I know that! Can't he put his tomatoes somewhere else?
MAVIS	I could suggest somewhere!
RICHARD	We all could, love!
VERA	Well let's just hang 'em here for now, or my arms are gonna drop off!

(VERA *goes to hang the baskets.*)

MAVIS	It's just that he'll say they're his hooks! If we could have left them in your conservatory for a little bit longer, Vera . . .
VERA	Well if it wasn't for Doug's birthday we could have, but I've got all t' family coming round; you know what it's like . . .
RICHARD	I think it's too warm in there now anyway; it's June and we needed to get them outside.
MAVIS	Could you not put some outside at your house?
RICHARD	We need to see them in situ, Mavis. Or I'm not going to get the right idea, am I?
MAVIS	He'll say he doesn't want them there, that's all.
VERA	I've got Doug coughing his guts up; it's his birthday, and he still hasn't shaken off his cold so I can't be worried about Stan's tomato hooks!
RICHARD	Have you tried him with Jasmine tea?
VERA	Jasmine tea? He can't eat curly lettuce, Richard, so that's definitely had it!
MAVIS	Well why don't you go, Vera, we'll finish off here.

VERA	I'll come and help with t' watering later on tomorrow if you like. And if you've any more trouble with next door, tell me; I'm in the bloody mood for her!
MAVIS	Well I've Richard here now; he'll look after me.
VERA	What's he gonna do? Try her tights on?
RICHARD	Go on; you cheeky bitch!
VERA	I bet Doug's going bloody blue with me being away. Mind you, it'll make a change; he usually goes red. See you!

(VERA *exits, as does* RICHARD, *who pulls two more pots of plants through the gate and takes the pots from the trolley.*)

RICHARD	I'll come and bring these in . . . (*From off stage.*) Tight squeeze, Mavis, isn't it?

(RICHARD *struggles on with another pot.*)

Now then, do we feed these now or what?

MAVIS	We'll do it tomorrow, then they'll do for another week.
RICHARD	Ooo, listen to you.
MAVIS	Well, I've been living with the King of the Hanging Baskets for most of my life, so . . . what are the labels for?
RICHARD	Colour coding.

(RICHARD *demonstrates.*)

These are the white ones blending into a pale pink, then on to these, which are deeper, and then moving across we go more purpley and into that cornflower blue.

MAVIS	I hope we've potted them right, because you can't always tell what colour they are at this stage.
RICHARD	Don't bloody say that now for God's sake, or my wave of colour's going to go all over the shop.
MAVIS	Fingers crossed, then!
RICHARD	I think it's time for another drink, don't you?
MAVIS	Not for me; I've tea to do. He'll go mad if it's not ready when he's back.
RICHARD	Just have a quick one. Takes the edge off!
MAVIS	I can't. Oh I can, go on then! It is nice, isn't it, with that bit of fruit in it.

(RICHARD *pours* MAVIS *a Pimm's*. MAVIS *considers her hands*.)

MAVIS	Look at my nails – ruined.
RICHARD	Mine are too!
MAVIS	Filthy. And my nail varnish, all but rubbed off.
RICHARD	I used to wear nail varnish!
MAVIS	How is it that doesn't surprise me, Richard?
RICHARD	When I was at college.
MAVIS	I sometimes wish I could have gone to college. Never got chance. It was never on the radar in our house.
RICHARD	I was lucky.
MAVIS	You were!
RICHARD	I think it was with my parents being arty, I suppose.

MAVIS	Mine weren't. I had to go and get a job, Richard; then they took all the money I brought in. Oh hell . . . when I think back! I thought that that was normal but . . .
RICHARD	I thought I was going to be famous. We all did in my group. None of us ever got anywhere close like! Except for Martin Jeavons; he had a thing with Elton John, or so they said, but . . .
MAVIS	Yes, well you had a bandana when I first met you.
RICHARD	Hey, I can believe that!
MAVIS	In fact you had a bandana when we did *Grease*.
RICHARD	How sad is that?
MAVIS	Very!
MAVIS	They had to sew me into that cat-suit; can you remember? I wouldn't get into it now.
RICHARD	I bet you would, though.
MAVIS	Be a bit bumpy!
RICHARD	Bumpy's good.
MAVIS	Do you think I could?
RICHARD	Well you've got no fat on you, have you.
MAVIS	Oh do you know something? I love you, Richard. You say all the right things.
RICHARD	I mean unlike me, who's as fat as a pig. Let's be honest, I was never Danny Zuko anyway, was I?
MAVIS	You weren't bad.
RICHARD	Oh, thanks for that.
MAVIS	But you're right, you're more Noël Coward.

RICHARD   Oh lovely.

               (*He starts to sing.*)

               "Mad dogs and Englishmen go out in the midday sun."

MAVIS   Oh, do it, Richard! Go on, do it!

RICHARD   (*as Noël Coward*) No, love!

MAVIS   Oh, darling, please do it!

RICHARD   Oh . . . if you insist!

MAVIS   Darling, I do!

RICHARD   Mad dogs and Englishmen go out in the midday sun.
               The toughest Burmese bandit can never understand it.
               In Rangoon the heat of noon is just what the natives shun
               They put their scotch and rye down, and lie down.
               In the jungle town where the sun beats down . . .

MAVIS   To the rage of man or beast

RICHARD   The English garb of the English sahib merely gets a bit more creased.

MAVIS   In Bangkok at twelve o'clock!

RICHARD   They foam at the mouth and run.

MAVIS   But Mad dogs and Englishmen . . .

RICHARD   Yes mad dogs and Englishmen.

BOTH   Go out in the midday
               Out in the midday
               Out in the midday.

RICHARD   Sun!

(STAN *has entered. He carries a large carrier bag and places it on the table.*)

STAN   What's going off?

MAVIS   Me and Richard were just having a laugh. Do you want a drink?

STAN   No I don't.

MAVIS   It's all gone anyway. Sorry, didn't think you'd be back home yet.

STAN   Came early to get out of t' car park.

RICHARD   Was it a good show?

STAN   It was alright.

MAVIS   You don't sound very enthusiastic.

STAN   It was too crowded, you couldn't see owt.

MAVIS   Well that's not so good, is it?

STAN   No, it wasn't.

MAVIS   Do you want a cup of tea and a biscuit instead?

STAN   No I'll wait for my meal, what we having?

MAVIS   I was going to do some chicken but . . .

STAN   Isn't it ready?

MAVIS   No, because you weren't supposed to be back until six. That was the time you said. Six! Everything ready for six you said!

STAN   But if you haven't even started it . . .

MAVIS   It'll be ready on the dot! Six o'clock.

RICHARD   We've got all the baskets and stuff done; it's been a job but . . .

MAVIS	What do you think?
	(STAN *looks around the garden.*)
STAN	Well you can't keep them there, they're for my little tomatoes.
MAVIS	They're just there for now.
STAN	Well they can't stay there.
MAVIS	I thought we could put some more hooks up on the shed. But we haven't got round to it, have we, Richard?
STAN	They'll be too heavy for t' shed.
MAVIS	No they won't.
RICHARD	Well couldn't you put your little tomatoes on the shed?
STAN	They'll not get as much sun.
MAVIS	I said he wouldn't like it.
STAN	I knew this would happen; I knew you'd bugger my garden up.
MAVIS	We're not, "buggering it up" are we, Richard?
	(*A beat*).
RICHARD	Well, I think it's about time I went, so I'm going to get off then, Mavis.
MAVIS	You don't have to.
RICHARD	No, no, I'd better. I've got to feed my cats and do one or two bits! Thanks for today, I've enjoyed it. Bye Stan; hey, if you do move them baskets, watch my labels. They're labelled so we know where we are. We don't want to get them all mixed up?
MAVIS	I'll see you later . . .

RICHARD	Alligator!
	(RICHARD *exits. It is icy between* STAN *and* MAVIS.)
MAVIS	I'd better get 'tea on then, I suppose.
STAN	I think you might need a cup of tea first.
MAVIS	I'm fine!
STAN	How long's he been here, then?
MAVIS	Oh, don't start . . .
STAN	He's never away!
MAVIS	Vera went and then we had a drink.
STAN	Didn't she want one?
MAVIS	Doug's not so well, so . . . (*A beat.*) And I've had a do with her next door and all, so don't start. Caught her roaming round.
STAN	What for?
MAVIS	Weren't you supposed to give her some plants? Because she thinks you were.
STAN	She's a bloody nuisance.
MAVIS	She thinks we don't like her.
STAN	Well I don't.
	(MAVIS *notices the bag* STAN *has brought.*)
MAVIS	What's in the bag, then?
STAN	Well I'd bought you sommat, but you're not interested.
MAVIS	How did you work that out?
STAN	Well you're not, are you?

MAVIS   I am.

STAN   You're drunk.

MAVIS   I'm not.

STAN   You'll not bloody like it anyhow.

MAVIS   Well I'll never know if I don't see it!

STAN   I don't think it's the right thing now.

MAVIS   Let me see it then.

STAN   No, it's all right.

MAVIS   Can't I at least have a look?

STAN   No, leave it.

MAVIS   For God's sake, what's the matter with you now?

STAN   You!

MAVIS   Oh shit to you then, I'm going to do t' tea.

STAN   Here then! Bloody have it. But it'll not be rate; nowt I do ever is.

(STAN *offers* MAVIS *the bag.*)

MAVIS   Do you want me to open it or not?

STAN   Please yourssen!

(MAVIS *delves into the carrier and produces a painted metal bucket of the kind one might find on a canal barge.*)

MAVIS   It's a bucket.

STAN   I know it's a bloody bucket!

MAVIS   Well . . . it's different!

STAN	I thought it might do for t' competition. It'd look good with some marigolds in.
MAVIS	It would, yes, yes it would!
STAN	Yes, well so . . .
MAVIS	The thing is though, Stan, we've done 'em all! We've potted up. We've nothing left to put in it.

(*Silence.*)

STAN	Well, I can give you some marigolds if you want.
MAVIS	I thought you'd none spare?
STAN	Well this is different, isn't it?

(*A beat.*)

MAVIS Well I don't think it'll go with Richard's theme, to be honest. We've got a theme, you see! We've, well . . . we've got a theme!

(*A beat.*)

But I do like it. It's just not right.

STAN	To me, flowers are flowers. They look nice whatever you plant 'em in.
MAVIS	Well that's not what we're doing, so . . .

(*A beat.*)

STAN	(*hurt*) I'll put the damn thing in t' soddin' bin, then!
MAVIS	I didn't say I didn't like it!
STAN	You didn't have to.

MAVIS	Can't we put it in that corner up by t' greenhouse?
STAN	Where no bugger'll see it?
MAVIS	It'll be nice there.
STAN	Jim'll have it; I'll give it to Jim. He right liked it.
MAVIS	Well why didn't he buy one, then?
STAN	I'll give it to Jim if you don't bloody well want it!
MAVIS	Well give it to bloody Jim then, you miserable sod.
	(MAVIS *starts to exit.*)
STAN	It's you who's miserable; I buy you a present and you throw it back in my face.
MAVIS	(*loudly*) It's a bucket Stan, it's a bloody bucket!
STAN	I know what it is!
MAVIS	And I did not throw it back in your face, I said that it wasn't right for the competition, that's all.
STAN	Bloody competition? Who do you think you are?
MAVIS	It's not want we want!
STAN	I knew this would happen.
MAVIS	Oh, don't start shouting tonight!
STAN	You're the one who's shouting!

MAVIS	Is there any wonder? Good grief man, I don't know what you want from me! Do you hear that? You're driving me around the bloody bend, with your buckets and your bloody bedding plants!
STAN	Yes, go on, shout; you're filling her mouth next door!
MAVIS	Do you know what? I'm not bloody well bothered. I'm not bothered about her and I'm not bloody bothered about you either!
STAN	Well thanks for that.
MAVIS	You and your buckets and you bloody moods!
STAN	This is with this sodding competition – it's taking over.
MAVIS	In fact I don't know why you bother coming home sometimes.
STAN	Well I'm going bed.
MAVIS	Good!
STAN	In the spare room!
MAVIS	Even better!
	(*A beat.*)
STAN	You're a mess, that's what you are; with your bloody arsey friends. A sodding mess and you always have been! I don't know who you think you are. I don't know why you can't just be bloody normal.
	(STAN s*torms off stage taking his bucket and the bag it came in with him.*)
MAVIS	What, like you? You're bloody normal are you, with your sodding canal boats and bloody

Jim for a mate? That's normal, is it? Well if that's normal thank God I'm not!

(*FX: The dog starts barking.*)

(MAVIS *remains on stage. She listens to the yapping dog for a while and then easily offers* . . .)

Oh shut up, you!

(*FX: The dog yaps until we hear* RIO *come and deal with it from off stage.*)

(MAVIS *stands and looks at the Pimm's. She drinks from the dregs of a couple of glasses and then puts all the empty glasses on a tray and slowly stands, but she is clearly a little worse for drink and is uneasy with the tray.*)

MAVIS   Oh . . . hell!

(MAVIS *makes her way off stage as the barking starts again. Throughout* RIO'S *offstage tirade* MAVIS *is swaying and moved to tears as she exits slowly.*)

(*Music. Lights. End of Act One.*)

ACT TWO

Scene One

The next morning. The patio is strewn with broken pots and a number of hanging baskets have been tipped over and emptied onto the patio. The door opens and MAVIS *enters with a bag of rubbish for the bin. On being confronted with the scene of destruction she stops in her tracks and drops the bag. There is the half-full watering can near the water butt.*

MAVIS   Oh God! (*Shouts.*) Stan!

         (MAVIS *attempts to rescue some of the plants and pots.* STAN *enters. He is slightly hung over.*)

STAN   What's up?

MAVIS   (*tearful*) Have you seen this?

STAN   Bloody hell!

MAVIS   What's been going on?

STAN   Bloody hell!

MAVIS   They're ruined, all my plants.

STAN   Bloody hell!

MAVIS   Is everything alright in your shed?

STAN   Eh?

MAVIS   Hadn't you better check? Hell, they've been all over the shop!

STAN   Well aren't we bloody well blessed?

         (STAN *enters his shed.*)

MAVIS   I can't believe it. All that work and now look at it!

(*She continues to try and rescue the plants.*)

Oh hell, I can't get my breath. Good grief!

STAN
: (*off*) It seems fine in here.

MAVIS
: You've been lucky then.

STAN
: (*off*) Nothing's been touched in here!

MAVIS
: You'd think it'd be first place they'd go.

STAN
: (*off*) No, everything's fine in here!

(STAN *comes out of the shed with a rubbish bag, a sweeping brush and a shovel.*)

MAVIS
: Oh I don't feel so well, to be honest.

STAN
: Well sit down for a minute.

MAVIS
: Look at it! It's a flaming disaster! Who'd do sommat like this? I mean what are they getting out of it if nowt's been taken?

STAN
: (*whispering to* MAVIS) You want to know what I think!?

MAVIS
: Who'd the bloody hell would do sommat like this, though?

STAN
: I think it's her next door.

(*A beat.*)

MAVIS
: Eh?

STAN
: Her.

MAVIS
: Give up?

STAN
: Well, I wouldn't be surprised.

MAVIS
: No, it . . .

STAN	I mean you had that "do" with her yesterday, didn't you?
MAVIS	I don't think she's got it in her, has she?
STAN	Well who else could it be?
MAVIS	Somebody that doesn't like my plants.
STAN	You're not wrong there!
MAVIS	Who the bloody hell?
STAN	It's her, now then I bet you – Bloody crackers! She's like death warmed up, creeping about.
MAVIS	It could be anybody, though.
STAN	Well it's not bloody me.
MAVIS	Nobody said it was? (*Noticing* STAN's *condition.*) You alright?
STAN	(*dismissive*) I've a splitting headache!
	(*A beat.*)
MAVIS	Why would she do it, though?
STAN	Eh?
MAVIS	Why would she do it?
STAN	They do, don't they, just to get at you. I've read about it in t' Telegraph. She's probably done one or two; now then, I bet you!
	(MAVIS *surveys the mess.*)
MAVIS	Well they've gone at it, whoever . . . !
STAN	Well like you said, she looked at our garden and was jealous to death.

MAVIS	She's not the vindictive type, though, is she?
STAN	How do you know?
	(MAVIS *closely inspects a hanging basket.*)
MAVIS	Look at all this! Everything ruined!
	(MAVIS *inspects further.*)
	Well, I'll tell you, if it is her, the police will find out.
STAN	Police?
MAVIS	Well, we'll have to report it, won't we?
STAN	They'll not be bothered about stuff like this.
MAVIS	'Course they will.
STAN	Nothing's been taken, has it? It's just vandalism, isn't it? That's what it'll go down as.
MAVIS	But stuff's been smashed.
STAN	That's what vandalism is! The police are just a waste of time; Jim had his shed broken into and a lathe taken and they did bugger-all. It's small fry to them.
MAVIS	You wouldn't be saying that if they'd broken in and taken your boat?
STAN	Well this is what I'm saying; nothing appears to be missing, does it?
MAVIS	Well I think we need to report it! Don't you?
STAN	Ring them then, but you'll have to leave it a mess until they've seen it. Could be days before they get round to sommat like this.

MAVIS	Oh, that's no good. I can't live with this!
STAN	Why don't I go round next door and have a word with her?
MAVIS	You can't do that, you can't just go round accusing somebody.
STAN	Well, I'll ask her if she heard owt. She's up to all hours, isn't she?
MAVIS	Well if you hadn't been in that spare room you might have heard sommat.
STAN	Hey, that was your fault, was that!
MAVIS	I'm surprised I didn't hear anything. I can't bloody well sleep in this weather.
STAN	Well you might have if you'd not been so bloody drunk!
MAVIS	Oh here we go; it'll be my fault in a minute. I'd better ring Richard and Vera; and its Doug's birthday an' all. What shall I say to them?
STAN	Say happy birthday to Doug!
MAVIS	What a pigging mess!
STAN	Well you can't do t' Village in Bloom competition now can you? That's put a bloody end to all that!
MAVIS	It depends how much we can save.
	(STAN *inspects the mess.*)
STAN	Well you've lost your pots and most of these plants are no good.

MAVIS	We've not checked 'greenhouse. I'd better go and have a look.
	(MAVIS *exits.* STAN *kicks a few plants into a pile and starts to put the bits of broken pot into the bin bag. He then gets the sweeping brush and starts to sweep up.* MAVIS *re-enters.*)
	That's all alright. But your tomatoes need watering.
	(*She notices that he is sweeping up the plants.*)
	What are you doing? I'm trying to save them; you've seen me trying to pick them up!
STAN	Give over, they're no bloody good now.
MAVIS	Some of them are. I'm not just throwing them away.
STAN	Mavis, they've bloody had it.
MAVIS	Just leave them.
STAN	They're broken.
MAVIS	Bloody leave them. They're my plants. I'll do it. They're my plants.
STAN	Oh alright, then, please your bloody self; they're only plants! I'm going to get a paper and a bloody Nurofen!
	(STAN *exits into the house.* MAVIS *stands centrally and surveys the detritus.*)
	(*Five minutes later. FX: Birdsong.* MAVIS *picks up the two tipped pots, gets the broom and starts to sweep up the peat.* RIO *enters. Throughout the scene* MAVIS *continues to sweep the rest of it up and puts it into the plastic bag.* RIO *enters carrying the peg bag.*)

RIO	I've brought your pegs back . . . They're all there. You can count 'em if you want.
MAVIS	They're the least of my worries. In fact I'm a bit upset, Rio, to be honest, so . . .
RIO	Well you would be, wouldn't you? When I saw him I thought should I do owt . . .
MAVIS	Eh?
RIO	But it's between you two, isn't it?
MAVIS	What is?
RIO	Well . . .
MAVIS	Did you say you saw somebody?
RIO	Well I can't sleep, you see . . .
MAVIS	Hey now, Rio . . . what's been going off?

(*A beat.*)

RIO	Well, my dad used to go off and break stuff.
MAVIS	Eh?

(RIO *looks around.*)

RIO	I was scared he was gonna throw sommat over t' fence.
MAVIS	Who?
RIO	Well . . . I don't like to say after he made me my rabbit box!
MAVIS	Stan?
RIO	Where is he?

MAVIS	He's got a headache! Gone for t' paper and a tablet!
RIO	Well it's him that should friggin' well sweep it up after all t' mess he's made. He's gonna be embarrassed now, isn't he? I bet he thought nobody could see him. I mean, no offence but my Granddad went weird! He thought he was Marilyn Monroe for two months.
MAVIS	Did he?
RIO	Shall I get another brush?
MAVIS	No, leave it.
RIO	I don't mind.
MAVIS	(*explosive*) JUST LEAVE IT!
RIO	I'm only . . .
MAVIS	Please.
RIO	I'll leave it, then.
MAVIS	Are you saying that Stan did this?
RIO	Well . . .
MAVIS	And you saw him?
RIO	Oh yeh, I saw him. He was going at it like a madman; thought he was going to have a friggin' heart attack. It's a wonder you didn't hear him, cursing and effing.
MAVIS	Are you sure?
RIO	What am I now, a frigging liar or sommat? You want to report him to the police for that! Somebody should.

(*A beat.*)

	Anyway – thanks for the pegs!
MAVIS	Oh it's no trouble that, Rio.
RIO	See you. Are you sure you don't want me to help?
MAVIS	No, it's all right, honestly. Thanks!

(RIO *exits through the gate.* MAVIS *is emotional and close to tears. Silence.* STAN *enters with the paper through the house. He stands on the step and calls to her.*)

STAN A load of rubbish in t' paper. Haven't you put kettle on yet?

(*A beat.*)

Mavis? Aren't we having a cup of tea?

(*A beat.*)

I think that rain might blow over.

(*A beat.*)

Mavis?

MAVIS	Rio's brought my pegs back.
STAN	That's good, then.
MAVIS	She can't sleep, she says.
STAN	Well she looks like a bloody zombie!

(*A beat.*)

MAVIS Why did you do it?

(STAN *reads the paper easily.*)

STAN   You what?

MAVIS   Why?

STAN   What's up now?

MAVIS   Why did you do it?

STAN   Do what?

MAVIS   You know what.

STAN   Eh?

MAVIS   I know it was you.

STAN   What?

MAVIS   She saw you.

STAN   Saw me what?

MAVIS   Breaking t' pots up; doing this.

STAN   She bloody didn't, though.

MAVIS   Well she says she bloody did!

STAN   You don't want to take any notice of her do you? She's a bloody half-wit!

MAVIS   She said she saw you do it, Stan.

STAN   She's heard you mention the police; she's panicking.

MAVIS   Police that you didn't want to get involved? She's on about reporting you.

STAN   You're barmy for even listening to her!

MAVIS   Am I?

STAN   You bloody are!

MAVIS	So why would she lie?
STAN	Why would I?
MAVIS	Why would she come round here and make it up?
STAN	Because she's bloody nuisance. The dog's allus barking; playing her music. Up till God knows when. She's a pissing nuisance, that's why – to get at us!

(STAN *makes to exit.*)

	Oh, I'm going in. Fancy believing her over me? Good grief, you come out with some stuff . . .
MAVIS	Well nothing's happened to owt of yours, has it?
STAN	Owt of mine?
MAVIS	Funny how your boat and your bloody bucket weren't touched!
STAN	Hey, I'm not having this.
MAVIS	Why did you do it, then?
STAN	I've done nowt!
MAVIS	Is it because you couldn't be in bloody charge? That's why you didn't want to join in with us, because you couldn't be in charge and you were scared of not winning!
STAN	Oh, here we go . . .
MAVIS	I mean you're such a bloody expert in everything that if we didn't win you'd be found out, wouldn't you? And when we did it without you, you didn't bloody like it. Is that it? You're like a big kid!

STAN	Well I'll not be fixing your scenery any more, then, if I'm like a big kid!
MAVIS	And I'm not going to dig your bloody onions, so . . . In fact I'll tell you something when I think about it; the flowers and veg get more bloody attention than me. Was I having too much of a laugh? Or was it because your tea wasn't ready on time? Or was it because our baskets were better than yours? Well they're definitely not now, are they?
STAN	She's caused all this; bloody Dracula next door! Pissing nuisance.
MAVIS	Is that why you did it?
STAN	It wasn't me!
MAVIS	Liar!
STAN	It wasn't!
MAVIS	Liar!
STAN	It wasn't!
MAVIS	Tell me the truth.
STAN	I'm telling you!
MAVIS	Tell me the truth, Stan.
STAN	I'm telling you!
MAVIS	Tell me the truth!
	(*A beat.*)
STAN	Alright!
	(*A beat.*)
	Alright! Bloody hell!

MAVIS	See! She saw you do it!
STAN	Satisfied?
MAVIS	Good God. Nobody would believe it if I told 'em. (*She starts to cry.*) My own husband . . . my own husband!
STAN	I'd had a couple of whiskies, and it got to me . . .
MAVIS	A couple? Is that why you've got thick head!
STAN	I had half a bloody bottle if you must know.
MAVIS	It's no excuse, is it?
STAN	It got to me . . . All your bloody parading, farting about. Bloody Richard prancing about, embarrassing me in my own back garden. Allus on . . . non stop "the show this, the show that". Hell-fire, take a battery out!
MAVIS	Why, because you want me to be sommat I'm not?
STAN	I just want to be put first for once.
MAVIS	And so do I!
STAN	Anyway . . . yes, hell, I did it. And I'm not proud!
MAVIS	Is that all you've got to say?
STAN	What do you want me to say?
MAVIS	Well how about a bloody apology for a start . . . (STAN *shouts loudly.*)
STAN	Alright, I'm sorry.

MAVIS Stop shouting!

STAN This is what you're like. I've said it. I'm sorry!

MAVIS Are you?

STAN 'Course I am; what do you think I am?

MAVIS Well I think it's too late!

STAN You've asked me to say sorry and I've said it!

MAVIS Well it's too bloody late for that.

STAN I was out of order. You can have some of my plants if you want.

MAVIS I don't want.

STAN I was daft, I know I was. I was bloody stupid.

MAVIS Well I don't want it any more.

STAN I've said I was daft it was just . . . I don't know!

MAVIS I can't go on like this, Stan. I don't want to. I don't want to live with a man who does this!

STAN Now, you're being daft now.

MAVIS No, I'm not. I mean it. I can't live with a man who does this to my plants. What will people say? What will people think! It's not normal behaviour. It's psychotic!

(*A beat.*)

STAN Hey, I'll go put kettle on, shall I?

MAVIS That's not going to change owt.

STAN	I'll make you a cup of tea.
	(*He exits into the house.* MAVIS *sits, distraught.* STAN *re-enters.*)
STAN	Where did you say you've put tea bags?
	(MAVIS *doesn't answer.*)
	I'll try another cupboard . . .
	(MAVIS *sits for a moment, then* RIO *enters.*)
RIO	Not seen my rabbit, have you?
MAVIS	Eh?
RIO	My rabbit . . . Friggin thing's escaped again . . . I saw it go but I couldn't catch it.
MAVIS	What's happened to your box?
RIO	I sold that to my mate. She thought it was mint!
MAVIS	Mint what?
RIO	Just mint . . . I'd better look for my rabbit missen'.
	(*She starts to wander off.* STAN *enters and stands on the doorstep.*)
STAN	There's no Tetley tea bags; do you want one of them with a bit of string on it?
MAVIS	Bloody hell.
RIO	Fluffy!
STAN	I'll do one of them then!
	(STAN *exits inside the house.*)

MAVIS	Bloody hell fire!
RIO	Fluffy? She's there, look.
MAVIS	Oh, God help me!

(RIO *follows Fluffy off stage.* MAVIS *exits through the house.*)

(*Lights. Music*)

Scene Two

Lights. STAN *enters from the house, crosses to the pond, looks at his watch. He crosses back to the house, adjusts a chair and exits to the house. Lights.*

Scene Three

The next day. Birdsong. STAN *enters from the house. He is wearing a different cardigan and is on the phone, waiting for it to connect him to a number. He walks and looks at his pond, then looks around the garden.*

STAN   What time does it end then, Jim? That's a long 'un, isn't it? I don't go, not anymore. I fell out with Gordon, can't you remember? No, I've had enough of Probus, Jim; it's full of people who like the sound of their own voice. He's got a good boat, has he? Well he's a big pond, hasn't he?

(STAN *walks down to his shed and tries the door.*)

No she's gone, still stopping up at Vera's. Of course I'm on my own at night! Hey that's not funny; I've got the grim reaper living next door. Listen, I've got some of them little French beers in, so . . .

(STAN *listens intensely.*)

Oh Gerald's coming round, is he? I thought you didn't like steam engines. And he's building it from scratch? Has he got all the pistons? That's going to take some doing, then! You're still on with yours, are you?

(STAN *sits lightly.*)

You know me. Nowt gets to me! What about tomorrow?

(STAN *stands and walks to the pond.*)

Your daughter's coming? A carvery, that should be nice, then! I'll probably see you at weekend then by the sound of . . .

(STAN *stands still.*)

Whitby? Oh right! She's got a caravan now, then? Oh it's lovely up there for a couple of days. A fortnight?

(STAN *smells the air, a faint whiff of smoke emanates from the back door and kitchen.*)

Well I'll have to let you go, Jim. I've got some toast on. Oh aye, washing, cooking . . . Alright, Jim. Have a good time, then.

(STAN *switches off the phone and makes his way towards the back door of his house as* VERA *enters the garden. There is a silence between them.*)

VERA	Still here?
STAN	Just about.
VERA	What's happening?
STAN	Nay Vera, you tell me. She won't even come to the bloody phone!

VERA	Well have you thought about coming up and talking to her?
STAN	I didn't walk out!
VERA	Hey listen, I've got Doug badly and a lodger now. I mean she's welcome but we're only up the road; this is bloody silly.
STAN	She's in her sixties and she's playing these tricks, Vera.
VERA	And what about you, throwing the bloody teddy out the cot?
STAN	She'll come back or she won't; it's that simple.
VERA	What are you getting out of this?
STAN	It's always me, Vera.
VERA	Well it is you, we all know that!
STAN	It's been coming has this!
VERA	And that's what you want, is it?
STAN	Bloody hell, Vera . . . you know want she's like; she gets bloody carried away!
VERA	Aye and you know what; some times you have to.
STAN	I'm going to get some breakfast on!
	(STAN *exits into the house.* VERA *is alone on stage, she calls after* STAN.)
VERA	Sometimes you have to get carried away in this life Stanley! Believe you me! I've been a carer nearly all my bloody life. Sometimes you have to get carried away.

(VERA *realises that* STAN *can not hear her. She follows him into the house.*)

Hey, you, can you bloody hear me? Or am I on your deaf side? Why don't you just put your pride away and go up and bloody see her? Can you hear me?

(VERA *exits into the house as the lights fade. Lights. Music.*)

Scene Four

The next evening. Fairy lights twinkle around STAN'S *shed. A number of concealed lights illuminate the area.* STAN *enters from the side of the house. He has a bunch of flowers with him, and has changed his jumper. He is clearly frustrated that* MAVIS *has not responded to his approach at* VERA'S. *He throws the flowers onto the patio table and unlocks the door, switches on the lights and then comes back out onto the patio with a can of beer. He is about to sit when he notices* RIO, *who has appeared from the bottom of the garden and is now sat by the pond. The atmosphere between them is tense and slightly absurd. She has been roaming around at the bottom of his garden once more.*

STAN What do you want?

RIO You been up to get her back, then? What with the flowers and that? I'd have thought they'd have been the last thing she wanted! What're you going to do now then, Stan?

STAN Mind my own business. Like you should.

RIO I saw you, you know.

STAN I bloody know that.

(RIO *indicates a skylight in her roof. A beat.*)

RIO	That box was good and all. I sold it, you know. Four quid.
STAN	Well you cheeky sod.
RIO	We could market them and sell them. There's a load of folks who'd buy sommat like that.
STAN	Well I don't know about that.
RIO	You could make a dog box and all, couldn't you?
STAN	Hey now, steady . . .
RIO	There's a lot of folks with dogs. I'd have one if you were making a dog box. I have to chain mine to the dustbin.
STAN	I know that.
RIO	If I had a dog box; you know, a kennel . . .
STAN	I'm making no bloody kennels . . . not at the moment. I made one for our Joanne, and that's going back!
RIO	My Gran used to say that you weren't any good round the house. But that you can make owt! Be funny if she goes first, she used to say. He'll be lost. Live in his shed!
STAN	I think it's time you went now, Rio . . .
RIO	There's a way through the bottom of the garden, did you know? There's a place in the hedges. I reckon that's where my rabbit got through,' cos every other place is fenced off, isn't it? You don't want anybody to get in!
STAN	Not if I can help it!

RIO	It's like a little secret, isn't it? You, your pond, your shed. It's like a little island, isn't it? I bet you thought that nobody could see you, didn't you?
STAN	That's right!
RIO	My Gran said she used to watch you and all. Oh aye, you can see everything you do from up there.

(RIO *goes to exit, then stops.*)

Hey, if she doesn't want them flowers, you know I'll have 'em. They'll be nice them in my kitchen.

(STAN *encourages her to go by offering the flowers.*)

STAN	Here you go then, Rio! Have 'em. I'm going to bed.

(STAN *goes to exit.* RIO *watches* STAN *move onto his doorstep, then she moves to the table to take the flowers. She smells them and looks at* STAN's *house. He stops as she speaks.*)

RIO	Thanks a lot! Hey, if you ever want a chat you know, you've only to ask 'cos I'm only next door, and I'm by myself and all, you know. If ever you want a chat . . .
STAN	Oh, right then.
RIO	You've only to say . . .
STAN	Night then!

(STAN *disappears into his home and locks the door. The patio lights are snapped out.*)

RIO	Yes. Night, night!

(*Music. Lights.*)

Scene Five

A day later. Birdsong. RICHARD *enters carefully through the side gate. he looks around the garden.*

RICHARD Hello! Hello?

(*FX: The dog barks loudly.*)

Stan, are you there?

(RICHARD *notices the can of beer that has been left on the table from the previous scene. He picks it up and puts it in the bin.*)

Oh dear!

(*Enter* STAN *from the house, in the same clothes but looking slightly more dishevelled than in the last scene. He brings out a tray with a microwave meal on it which is still in its carton.*)

Stanley?

STAN Bloody hell, what you doing?

RICHARD I knocked.

STAN I need a bolt on that gate.

RICHARD Knocked a few times, but you couldn't have heard me.

STAN I was making my dinner.

RICHARD Looks nice.

STAN It stinks, I think it's got bloody garlic in it. I hate garlic. Can't stand t' smell.

RICHARD What did you get it for, then?

STAN   I didn't know it had bloody garlic in it, did I? I thought it was just bolognaise.

RICHARD Bolognaise always has garlic in it.

STAN   Mavis' bolognaise doesn't. It's no good, I can't eat that.

RICHARD Sounds like you need her back.

STAN   I've asked her, but she won't so sod her!

RICHARD Aye, well that's why I've come.

STAN   Oh aye?

RICHARD Have a man to man.

STAN   Oh aye?

RICHARD I mean I know you don't think much of me.

STAN   I've never said that.

RICHARD You don't have to. I've known you for years; you're the most miserable sod I've ever met.

STAN   Hey . . .

RICHARD Oh shut up, you silly old fart.

STAN   Not in my own bloody property.

RICHARD I'm surprised you didn't smash that up!

STAN   Hey, I'm not having it, Richard.

RICHARD Ooo calm down for God's sake, and listen for once. Mavis is now staying up with me at my house.

STAN   What?

RICHARD	Because Doug's feet are swelling up.
STAN	Bloody hell? What's going on?
RICHARD	And she was in the way, apparently.
STAN	Well how big has his feet bloody got?
RICHARD	Massive, by all accounts! But I'll tell you this, she's not happy, Stan.
STAN	Well she's not on her own there. I'm not happy with her stopping at your house! What she's playing at?
RICHARD	She's only going to stop for a couple of months.
STAN	She's bloody not, though?
RICHARD	Well I think you both need a break!
STAN	She's bloody not stopping for a couple of months, Richard. Hell fire!
RICHARD	Give yourselves a bit of space.
STAN	I'm not having that!
RICHARD	Excuse me, but I'm only trying to help here.
STAN	She's never wanted space before.
RICHARD	Well I'm only thinking about her feelings.
STAN	It's bloody embarrassing her staying with you for one night as far as I'm concerned. What the bloody hell does it say about me when my wife's living with you?
RICHARD	Why, what are you saying?
STAN	Never mind what I'm saying.

RICHARD	Hey, I am trying to help here!
STAN	I'll come round and bloody get her. I can't have that. Good grief, she'll fill everybody's mouth on the sodding estate!
RICHARD	Oh, lighten up!
STAN	I'll come up and get her.
RICHARD	Well good luck – because the way she's feeling at the moment, you'll be lucky if she ever wants to come back at all!
STAN	It's all talk!
RICHARD	I don't think it is. I think she bloody well means it, Stan. If you don't change I think she's gone for good. So you can get your frigging head around that. You've no idea how much you've hurt her.
STAN	It was nowt was that.
RICHARD	Is that what you think?
STAN	She's overreacting; She's been involved with t' amateur dramatics for too long!
RICHARD	Mavis is a vibrant woman Stan, she needs watering. If you don't water people they dry up. They're like your plants.
STAN	Well aye, but . . . ?
RICHARD	I mean she was really excited when I took her for a cappuccino yesterday, bless her. A cappuccino; how sad is that?
STAN	Bloody cappuccinos now!
RICHARD	And do you know why? Because when she's out with you she's not allowed one. You've

	told her it's cheaper for her to make a coffee when you get home.
STAN	Well it is, isn't it?
RICHARD	Can't you see what you're doing?
STAN	Oh aye, It'll all be me.
RICHARD	Listen, I don't talk much about it, but do you remember Peter, the guitarist?
STAN	No, not really.
RICHARD	He was in the band for *Joseph*; he was miserable, criticised everything I did. And even though I thought a lot about him, I left him, just took off, I'd had enough. When he got poorly, I went to visit him, but he was just the same. I got him t' wrong grapes, wrong book, wrong everything. I only went once. I thought, sod him, miserable mare. When he died he'd left me a note. His sister posted it to me. It said how much he thought about me, how much I made him laugh. Couldn't say it when he was alive, just couldn't say it.

(*A beat.*)

It was Mavis and Vera that got me through it, bless 'em, because it shook me up, still does. It seemed such a bloody waste. And that's what's upsetting me, because I don't want you and Mavis to end up like that.

(RICHARD *has become emotional.*)

STAN	Oh I'll get us a drink. Hell-fire, Richard!
RICHARD	No, you're alright, I'll get one. Have you a tissue?
STAN	On t' window bottom.

(RICHARD *goes into the house.* STAN *struggles with what to say.*)

STAN: (*shouting off to* RICHARD) You say Doug's feet's swelling up?

RICHARD: (*off*) Like balloons.

STAN: That's not so good, then.

(*A beat.*)

RICHARD: (*off*) You've let it get a mess in here, haven't you?

STAN: I haven't got round to it.

RICHARD: (*off*) Can't you even stack the dishwasher?

STAN: I don't know how it works. I've not managed to sort it out.

RICHARD: (*off*) And you a mechanic?

STAN: Anyway it costs more, doesn't it, running t' dishwasher? I'm better off washing up.

RICHARD: (*off*) Well you are if you do it.

STAN: It'll get sorted.

RICHARD: (*off*) There's a glass of sherry, that's all I can find.

STAN: It's from Christmas, is that.

RICHARD: (*off*) Bloody sherry, it went out with t' Ark!

STAN: Christmas came after t' Ark?

RICHARD: (*off*) Do you want one?

STAN: Not for me.

(RICHARD *enters carrying a schooner of sherry.*)

RICHARD   Anyway, I've said my piece, so . . .

STAN   I mean she's gone before, Richard, but after a few hours she allus come back.

RICHARD   Well what you did was just animal, wasn't it? Bloody primal, I think . . .

STAN   Hey, I'm not proud of missen.

RICHARD   It takes some getting over does something like that. It was her thing. She needs to be able to express herself or she'll . . . well, she'll stagnate, won't she? It's how we are.

STAN   Don't you think it's same for me? Since I got made redundant what else have I got? This little bit of bloody garden and my boats. When I was working I could mend any car they brought in and I'd send 'em back, as good as new. Job done! I had a purpose!

RICHARD   Hey don't knock 'em, Stan; them boats are good.

STAN   Well nobody sees 'em, though.

RICHARD   Well why don't you put them in a show, then?

STAN   Because the truth is they're not good enough. I haven't got the right tackle, and do you know why, because I can't afford it. They're just sommat to do. They're a project. And now I've done 'em I'm in bloody free fall! Pottering about, watering my greenhouse! Watching things grow; knowing that I'm getting older.

RICHARD   Oh we could all say that. Don't.

STAN   Mavis doesn't worry about stuff like that, she's a bloody ostrich. I wish I could be, but I can't. That's why I like a routine; keep my

| | mind active. When I come out of the routine, I'm lost in a fog. And when she starts going off to do shows, my routine goes to pot and I start panicking! It all comes in on me! Hell fire, we've had us ups and downs, but what will I do if I'm ever poorly? Sometimes I think I'm having a heart do when she's out. I just want her to value me, Richard, that's all. |

RICHARD   Hey come on, you silly mare . . .

(RICHARD *tentatively goes to hug* STAN. *Enter* RIO, *who catches them hugging.*)

STAN   Whooah, easy, Richard. Bloody hell!

(STAN *and* RICHARD *are frozen mid-embrace.* RIO *has brought in a supermarket carrier with food in it.*)

RIO   Hey, don't mind me, that's what my granddad fought for, it's a free country! Got some more of that bolognese there for you and some milk. It was seven pounds sommat but I've kept change for going; is that alright? You just carry on, I'll stick this in your fridge then; is that alright?

(RIO *makes her way into* STAN'S *house.*)

RICHARD   I'll help you get her back.

(RICHARD *lets go of* STAN *and exits through the gate.* STAN *picks up glass.*)

(*Music. Lights.*)

Scene Six

MAVIS *stands by the pond. She looks around the garden; she is reluctantly content.*

MAVIS	(*loudly*) Can you remember when we had fish in here? (*Partly to herself.*) That's going back! I never thought we'd live in a bungalow either. That's a bloody shock. Sign of the times, Stanley!
	(*Slowly, she moves and looks at the garden.*)
	Close today! Oppressive.
	(*A beat.*)
	Look at this garden. It's tiny really, isn't it?
	(*She slowly moves to sit at the patio table where everything from the previous scene has been removed. As she settles,* STAN *enters with a cup of tea which he gives to* MAVIS.)
STAN	There's your tea. No sugar. Your toast'll be here in a minute. Only I can't do tea and toast, not at same time. I've done some toast, but I've burnt it. So I've put some more in. Shall I butter it?
MAVIS	Well I don't want it dry, do I?
STAN	I'll butter it then. I can't find t' jam.
MAVIS	Top of t' fridge.
STAN	That's gone off. What about Marmite?
MAVIS	I hate marmite.
STAN	Hang on, I've got to get back to my toast.
	(*He re-enters the house.*)
	Oh bloody hell. Not again!
MAVIS	I can't wait for my Sunday dinner.
STAN	(*from off*) Don't worry. It's all under control!

MAVIS	Can I have marmalade, do you think?
STAN	(*off*) I'm dealing with this.
MAVIS	What's it doing? Taking over t' kitchen?
STAN	(*off*) I've done it . . .
MAVIS	Great.
STAN	(*off*) It's coming . . .
	(STAN *enters from kitchen with a very small piece of buttered toast on a plate. The edges of the toast have been removed.*)
STAN	Here we are.
MAVIS	Has it shrunk?
STAN	I cut edges off, they got a bit burnt and all.
MAVIS	Well that's not going to fill me up.
STAN	I thought you were on a diet?
MAVIS	I don't know what made you think that!
STAN	I can do you some more if you want?
MAVIS	No, I haven't got time.
STAN	It's the thought that counts.
MAVIS	And what thought is this?
STAN	I thought I could do it, but it's harder than you think.
MAVIS	Well you can try again tomorrow, can't you? Practise makes perfect. Are you getting me some marmalade, or what?

STAN	Bloody hell!
	(STAN *goes back into the house.*)
MAVIS	Now you know how I feel!
STAN	(*off*) I'm not as bossy as you are.
MAVIS	You bloody are though!
STAN	(*off*) Well I've tidied up.
MAVIS	You bloody haven't! Five days I've been away, and you've managed to turn it into a tip.
	(STAN *enters with the marmalade.*)
STAN	I've been struggling with t' Hoover, to be honest.
MAVIS	You just plug it in and push it.
STAN	Brush is too short though. They must have made it for a dwarf.
MAVIS	Well did you think of extending it?
	(MAVIS *attempts to eat the toast.*)
STAN	I only tried it once. I was bent over like Quasimodo!
	(STAN *goes back into the house.*)
STAN	(*off*) Did you miss me, then?
MAVIS	No I bloody didn't.
STAN	(*off*) What you come back for, then?
MAVIS	Richard talked me into it. He was worried about you. And anyway I couldn't stay there forever, it just wasn't fair.

(STAN *comes onto the patio with a tea towel.*)

STAN Got fed up of him, did you?

MAVIS No! We were having a great time.

STAN Drinking coffee chinos?

MAVIS Cappuccinos!

STAN You'll have paid through nose for them.

MAVIS Well it's as near to Italy as I'll get, so . . . And we went to a jazz club.

STAN He never said.

MAVIS And an art exhibition.

STAN Oh right!

MAVIS In Leeds. All these things made of glass, it was lovely. And he didn't rush me; you always rush me. I never get a chance to look at anything with you, not even in t' supermarket. We've got to get back for t' tomatoes or Jim ringing to talk about your boat. It's like being in t' army!

STAN Bloody jazz club and all, then.

MAVIS And I'll tell you sommat; if you went you'd enjoy it. We could go one night with Richard.

STAN What sort of jazz is it?

MAVIS Bloody jazz, jazz!

STAN Well I . . .

MAVIS Oh, don't sound so enthusiastic! This is the trouble – Richard's full of energy, he wants to share things, go places – but you?

STAN Aye, he would be.

MAVIS   And thank God he is, or where would I be? I'll tell you sommat – he's a good friend to me is Richard.

STAN   What and I'm not? After all I do?

MAVIS   You've made me one slice of toast! And you've had two goes at that!

STAN   Hey . . .

MAVIS   You're my husband, Stan, but you're not my friend any more! That's the truth. You used to be.

STAN   Hey, we used to have a laugh.

MAVIS   Used to!

STAN   I mean there's nowt to laugh about though now, is there?

MAVIS   Yes, but why are you such a miserable sod?

STAN   It's just crept up on me.

MAVIS   Well I don't want it to creep up on me! I mean you never want to talk anymore either, do you?

STAN   What is there to talk about?

MAVIS   Everything!

STAN   What do you want me to do; keep bleating on about why they sold off the garage and I lost my job? You'd soon get fed up of that.

MAVIS   I mean you make them boats and you won't show 'em to anybody.

STAN   Oh, don't you start on that.

MAVIS   I don't know what's up with you sometimes.

STAN	I feel useless, that's what's up with me. Useless, because nobody needs me, not even you!
MAVIS	But you're not useless, are you? You're good at loads of stuff.
STAN	Nowt that you're interested in.
MAVIS	What does that matter?
STAN	Because I want us to do stuff together.
MAVIS	Well you used to come and do the scenery at 'Parish Players. Why did you stop doing that?
STAN	I want to do stuff with just you, not every bugger and t' vicar's wife.
MAVIS	But I like company, Stan. That's me; I like to be in company. That's who I am.
STAN	And I don't. And that's who I am!
MAVIS	You won't even try, though.
STAN	It's you that doesn't try for me.
MAVIS	You must be joking.
STAN	You could have come to t' boat show.
MAVIS	You didn't want me to.
STAN	'Course I did. Do you think I like going with silly Jim? You think I'm tight. He sucks mints all day so he doesn't have to buy a cup of tea.
MAVIS	Well I never knew you wanted me to come.
STAN	This is why I get cheesed off with you!
MAVIS	What, because you're jealous of me being with Richard and Vera?

STAN   Yes, yes I bloody am!

MAVIS   Give up?

STAN   I'm nearly seventy, Mavis, and I'm bloody jealous!

          (*A beat.*)

          There, I've said it. I'm jealous because you have a better time with them than me.

MAVIS   Because they make me feel alive. You don't.

STAN   I used to.

MAVIS   I know you used to, so what's happened to that Stan? The truth is you can't be arsed to make the effort, and that's what Richard and Vera do, they make the bloody effort, Stan!

STAN   Hey, I am trying, you know.

MAVIS   Are you, are you really, though?

STAN   I'm fed up with missen, to be honest.

MAVIS   I can see that. Well I'm warning you, if you do owt like that again, that's it, finished. Richard's asked me if I want to go to Sitges and I could, easily; and then I might not ever come back.

STAN   You don't mean that though, do you?

MAVIS   Just bloody try me, Stan! Just bloody try me!

          (*Music. Lights.*)

Scene Seven

A few weeks later. The day of the "Village in Bloom" competition. RICHARD *enters with a stand for hanging baskets which he erects by the pond. He then starts stringing up bunting.* VERA *enters from the path that leads to the greenhouse with two enormous hanging baskets. They are impressive, in full bloom and display a mixture of plants and colours.*

VERA	Here, Richard, stop farting about and tell me where I'm going with these.
RICHARD	Over by the pond.
VERA	Chuff me, they're heavy.
RICHARD	I'm having everything focused on the pond.
VERA	Stan's idea that, wasn't it?
RICHARD	No.
VERA	That's what Mavis said.
RICHARD	It was me that came up with the nautical theme.
	(VERA *struggles to hang them on a "T" bar near the pond.*)
VERA	Oh hell . . .
RICHARD	Be careful with 'em, we've lost one lot; we don't want to lose any more.
VERA	I am being careful.
RICHARD	You could have fooled me.
VERA	There, they look good do them.
RICHARD	I wouldn't have gone for all them colours; it's too much of a mish-mash but . . .
VERA	We're lucky we've got some.

RICHARD	Well he couldn't not give us them, could he? In fact it was probably his plan all along. Now he's got it all how he wants. Bloody manipulative, I tell you!
VERA	Doug would never have done 'owt like that.
RICHARD	Is he any better?
VERA	His feet have gone down but he's got repetitive strain injury.
RICHARD	How's he got that, then?
VERA	Over-usingthe TV remote.

(*He finishes hanging the bunting.*)

RICHARD	Are you going to get them other pots?
VERA	Not by my bloody self I'm not.
RICHARD	Can't we ask t' next door to help us?
VERA	She's gone away. Taken t' dog and all, Mavis said. I hope she has it put down!
RICHARD	There is a God!
VERA	So come on!
RICHARD	I'm the bloody designer.
VERA	Well design your chuffin' self to come and help!
RICHARD	Where's Stan and Mavis? You wouldn't get Alan Titchmarsh doing this.

(VERA *and* RICHARD *exit down the garden.* STAN *enters from his shed, carrying a lighthouse, whistling. He ducks under the bunting, puts the lighthouse in a prominent place beside the pond.* MAVIS *enters from the kitchen carrying the painted bucket that* STAN *bought her earlier. It is now full of plants. She notices the lighthouse.*)

MAVIS	What the hell's that?
STAN	It's a lighthouse.
MAVIS	I know it's a lighthouse, but what's it doing there?
STAN	Being a lighthouse.
MAVIS	On a canal?
STAN	It's not a canal, it's a pond.
MAVIS	But the theme's a canal.
STAN	Bloody themes my arse.
MAVIS	It's what we agreed – barges, buckets and . . .
STAN	Bunting? What's that got to do with canals?
MAVIS	Hey you promised you'd keep your mouth shut!
STAN	I'll put it back in t' shed.
MAVIS	No, leave it.
STAN	Make your bloody mind up.
MAVIS	Let's wait and see what he says.
STAN	You know why Richard's chosen nautical, don't you? There's no surprise there, is there?
MAVIS	Hey, I'm warning you, not a word!
STAN	I'll get my other stuff. You'll probably not want that, either.

MAVIS	Not if it's another bloody lighthouse!
	(STAN *exits into the shed. We hear the sound of a drill.* RICHARD *and* VERA *enter laden with pots of plants.*)
VERA	Coming through!
RICHARD	Watch my feet!
VERA	I like these better than t' baskets!
	(*She notices the lighthouse.*)
	Hey up, look at this!
	(RICHARD *spots the lighthouse.*)
RICHARD	Is it a joke? Or has he made Grace Darling as well?
MAVIS	He might have.
VERA	It's lovely is that.
RICHARD	No, it's not.
VERA	Well I'd like to see you make one.
MAVIS	I know it's a bit . . .
RICHARD	Tacky I think is the word you're searching for!
VERA	It's well made is that.
RICHARD	It's totally wrong, though. A lighthouse, where are we?
VERA	Well it's nautical!
RICHARD	It's too Disney, though, Vera!

VERA	Well you can't not use it, not after all that effort he's put in. Bloody keep it, it's not doing any harm.
RICHARD	I'm sorry but if you keep that, I'm going to have to stand down as designer.
VERA	Chuffin' hell, Richard, it's Village in Bloom, not Chelsea Flower Show.
RICHARD	I know that and I want to sodding win!
MAVIS	I'll have a word with him.
RICHARD	I knew he'd try and take over.
VERA	We're supposed to be working as a team.
RICHARD	You want to be telling Stan that.
VERA	That lighthouse might be just what we need.
	(STAN *enters from the shed. He proudly carries his boat, which is filled with flowers.*)
STAN	What do you think of that then? That's bloody nautical, isn't it?
	(*A beat.*)
	Well say sommat!
	(*Silence.*)
	There's nobody else gonna have one of these.
RICHARD	Well, you're not wrong there.
VERA	I'll tell you what Stan; you've pushed chuffin' boat out with that!
STAN	Let's just hope it still sails!

MAVIS	You're never going to put it on t' pond are you?
STAN	'Course I am, this is your centre piece, this.
RICHARD	It's slightly Jeff Koons, so it just might work . . .
	(STAN *sails the boat.*)
STAN	Right, here we go . . . There, look . . .
VERA	It's not 'Titanic, is it?
RICHARD	No it's a barge, Vera.
	(*Silence. They all watch the event.*)
MAVIS	Well it's staying up.
STAN	It should do.
MAVIS	Worst bloody luck!
VERA	Fantastic that, Stan.
STAN	(*proudly*) Ar, I'm not bad at boats.
VERA	Fantastic, isn't it?
RICHARD	What can you say?
MAVIS	I think we all need a drink?
VERA	A bottle of Rum, eh, Stan?
RICHARD	A jug of Pimm's, Pimm's on the patio, we might as well go the whole hog.
	(RICHARD *exits with* MAVIS.)
RICHARD	Do you have any show CDs, Mavis?
MAVIS	Somewhere.

RICHARD	I've just had a thought.
	(MAVIS *and* RICHARD *exit into the house.* STAN *watches them.*)
VERA	Alright then? You and Mavis?
STAN	Ar.
VERA	It's always been easier to carry on than start again, Stan. If you start again you only end up in t' same place.
STAN	Hell, I'm out of breath. I'm falling to bits, Vera.
VERA	We all are; look at Doug. You've got make most of it, you're a long time dead.
STAN	Cheers for that. That's cheered me up.
VERA	I'll tell you sommat though, Stan, this looks chuffin' brilliant.
STAN	Well, we'll see what the judge has to say!
	(RICHARD *appears in the doorway carrying a CD player which just about reaches outside.*)
RICHARD	Just about reaches.
VERA	It won't be long now!
RICHARD	Final touches, Vera, then we're there.
VERA	What's that for, then?
RICHARD	Ambience.
VERA	Oh we're having some ambience and all, are we?
RICHARD	Set the mood.
VERA	Why don't you just concentrate on t' flowers?

RICHARD	Oh shut up, you.
	(*Enter* MAVIS *from the house with a jug of Pimm's and glasses.*)
MAVIS	Here we are, just a little one. I don't know about you two, but I'm all over t' place.
VERA	Well it's a big thing, isn't it? I mean, to rescue it all in just three weeks is a chuffin' miracle; we should get a medal for that!
MAVIS	Where's Stan?
	(*FX: A car arriving on the street outside.*)
VERA	Taken trolley back to t' greenhouse.
RICHARD	Is that a car?
VERA	I'll have a look see if it's them.
MAVIS	Oh God, they're' early. Who is it again?
VERA	(*going to the gate to peek through*) They said it was somebody from council.
MAVIS	Where the bloody hell is he?
VERA	It's a big car.
RICHARD	Shall I put the music on?
MAVIS	I can't believe they're this early.
RICHARD	Probably got a lot to get through.
	(STAN *appears.*)
MAVIS	Where've you been?
STAN	Watering my tomatoes.

MAVIS	Now?
STAN	Well I thought what if anybody wants to look at them?
MAVIS	They won't.
VERA	Hey, it's her. Chuffing hell! She's got a bloody hat on and everything!
RICHARD	If I'd have known, I could have worn my bandana.
VERA	Oh hell fire!
MAVIS	What's up?
VERA	It *is* her!
	(*She comes away from the gate.*)
RICHARD	Who?
VERA	Bloody Mayor. Vicky Feather!
RICHARD	It's not?
VERA	It bloody is!
MAVIS	Well that's brilliant, isn't it; we'll never win 'owt now!
RICHARD	We need music, music to help set the scene.
	(RICHARD *goes to the back door. We hear the voice of* VICKY FEATHER *from behind the gate.*)
VICKY	(*off*) Hello!
MAVIS	(*false truth*) Helloooo!
VICKY	(*off*) Are you there?

MAVIS — Come in! (*To* STAN.) Fasten your cardigan, Stan.

(MAVIS *opens the gate.*)

Hello!

(*Enter* VICKY FEATHER. *She is wearing an immaculate suit, with matching shoes and hat. She carries a clipboard and a handbag.*)

VERA — Hello! Oh this is nice, isn't it? Isn't it lovely? You wouldn't have thought you'd have as much garden would you, not with size of the house! It's a sun trap is this, Mavis! Isn't it lovely? A patio, a pond. Lovely!

(RICHARD *offers his hand.*)

RICHARD — Richard, hello!

VICKY — You were with the Parish Players!

RICHARD — I was.

VICKY — And Edna!

VERA — Vera.

(*It is pregnant and awkward with the mayor.*)

MAVIS — And do you know Stan?

VICKY — So this is the team?

MAVIS — And this is the display.

(*They walk over towards the pond.*)

VICKY — And how's Joanne doing?

VERA — She lives in Italy, doesn't she, Mavis?

VICKY — Does she?

MAVIS	She's a lawyer.
VERA	Yes, she's lawyer isn't she, Mavis?
VICKY	You must be very proud.
	(*They look at the exhibit. Silence.* VICKY *considers her notes.*)
VICKY	(*lost*) Well it's very different, isn't it?
RICHARD	It's a fusion of styles! Part pop art! Part kitsch! I mean it looks like Grace Darling meets Gracie Fields, but we thought, let's have some fun with it! Let's be different, mix it up lets celebrate with colour! Because flowers can give people so much joy, can't they?
VICKY	And this little section here, this is it, is it? This little bit round the pond?
MAVIS	This is it, yes!
VICKY	It doesn't strictly fit into a category, does it?
MAVIS	Well we're supposed to be in for t' best container garden.
VICKY	No, it's one container or one hanging basket? That's what it says on your form. I can only judge one.
STAN	Well you can't just judge these hanging baskets? They're all part of the display. If I'd have just been doing hanging baskets I would have done some bigger than these!
VICKY	Well you've entered under the one container section, haven't you?
RICHARD	You did actually read the form, didn't you, Vera?

VERA	I just filled in "container section", so . . .
STAN	There must be some kind of display section?
VICKY	Well there's "Best Public House" or "Community Group".
MAVIS	Well you can put us down as t' Parish Players display, can't you?
VICKY	No, because I can't just swap a category like that. Rules are rules, I'm afraid.
STAN	Oh rules my arse.
MAVIS	So what are you saying, that you can't judge us?
VERA	I thought you said, you could judge one container?
VICKY	Well yes, I can, but . . .
MAVIS	So you can judge the boat then, can't you?
VICKY	Well I can't really!
MAVIS	Why not!?
VICKY	Because it's not a container, is it? It's a barge, isn't it?
MAVIS	Well if a barge isn't a container I don't know what it is! That's what barges are, containers. Everybody knows that, they're up and down canals full of stuff. This one's full of flowers!
VICKY	But in fairness to you there aren't many flowers in it, are there? I mean I can't judge the barge, I can only judge what's in it, if that's what you're wanting me to judge. I mean the barge is good, but . . .
MAVIS	Good?

VICKY	Well it is!
MAVIS	Good?
VICKY	Well it is! Nobody's saying it isn't good!
MAVIS	It's more than bloody good!
VICKY	Well it is, you're right . . .
MAVIS	Good?
VICKY	No, it's very good, to be honest!
MAVIS	It ought to bloody be!
VICKY	Well it is!
MAVIS	Have you any idea how long it's taken him to make it?
VICKY	A long time, I dare say . . .
MAVIS	Have you any idea how many hours he's been working on it?
STAN	Hey, Mavis?
MAVIS	It's more than good; in fact if some of the houses your husband throws up were finished as good as that you could count yourself bloody lucky!
RICHARD	Oh here we go!
MAVIS	The bloke's a bloody craftsman!
VICKY	Well I haven't come to . . .
MAVIS	He's not just been brought in from Poland for six months; he earned this skill here! And do you know what your husband did? Shall I tell you?

VICKY	I don't think we need to get personal!
MAVIS	We bloody do, though!
STAN	Hey now!
MAVIS	He bought the garage that Stan had worked at all his life so he could build some more bloody rabbit hutches on the land! That's what he did. So don't come here patronising us saying it's bloody "good". Look at the detail in it! Look at the craft in it!
VICKY	Well I can understand . . .
MAVIS	I can't believe you've got the cheek to come into my own back garden and say it's just "good"! That's a work of sodding genius, that is! And I'll tell you this and all while I'm on . . . your dancers at Miss Feather's are a bloody disgrace, aren't they, Richard?
RICHARD	I'm saying nothing!
MAVIS	Aren't they, Vera.

(VERA *goes to say something* . . .)

MAVIS	I saw 'em in the Lord Mayor's parade, and they were all over the shop! And we've been kicked out of the Church Hall for them; it's bloody scandalous!

(MAVIS, *in tears, storms into her house.*)

It just is!

(STAN *is about to follow her.*)

STAN	Well?

(*A beat.*)

RICHARD	Well anyway!

STAN	She's never said owt like that about my boat before like, so . . . I wasn't even sure she liked it!

(*A beat.*)

I'll just pop and . . .

(STAN *exits. Silence.*)

VERA	So when will you let us know, then?
RICHARD	Bloody hell, Vera, smell the coffee!

(*A beat.*)

VICKY	Well it is a good boat, there's no doubt about it! But I just couldn't judge the boat, it wouldn't have been fair. I mean it's a lovely display!

(*A beat.*)

I'd better get away. I've got all Green Lane to do today, and the Star and Garter have entered thirty hanging baskets. I think they've gone mad up there. Nice to meet you; maybe you could enter next year! Sorry! Bye!

(VICKY *exits easily. Silence.*)

VERA	Looked good and all, didn't it?
RICHARD	What a bloody farrago!
VERA	I think it looked good!
RICHARD	She was just being awkward.
VERA	Did you see her dancers? I'm no lightweight, Richard, but I could do better my bloody self. Maybe we should have stuck to doing shows, you know.

(*A beat.*)

RICHARD	Yes, I think so, Vera, because that lighthouse is a bloody disaster!

(*A beat.*)

VERA	'Cos there's no business like show business, Richard, is there?

(*A beat.*)

RICHARD	You're not wrong, Vera! No, you're not wrong!

(*Music. Lights.*)

Scene Eight

Six weeks later. Birdsong. The garden is still in full bloom and the bunting remains up. STAN *enters from the house with a cup of tea and some digestives.*

STAN	Here we are! Cup of tea and a digestive. Mavis! Come on, tea's up!

(MAVIS *enters from the path that leads to the greenhouse. She is carrying a bowl of tomatoes.*)

MAVIS	I've been picking tomatoes. Look at them, they smell gorgeous. We're getting bowl after bowl of 'em now.
STAN	It's been a good crop.
MAVIS	'Way its going we're gonna have to give some away.
STAN	No, don't do that, we don't want to be giving 'owt away. Can't we freeze 'em?
MAVIS	I suppose so. And 'onions have grown bloody enormous, haven't they?

STAN	That's with all that compost we dug in.
	(STAN *picks up the watering can and moves down towards the pond.*)
MAVIS	That I dug in, you mean?
STAN	Sit down and get your cup of tea.
	(MAVIS *puts the tomatoes on the table and sits.*)
MAVIS	Aren't you having one?
STAN	I've had one; I need to water all this.
	(*He swerves to avoid the bunting.*)
STAN	Can't we take this bloody stuff down?
MAVIS	No, I like it, it makes me happy.
STAN	It's not gonna last much longer.
MAVIS	Well when it falls to bits we'll pull it down. It's not a bad cup of tea is this.
	(*Enter* VERA. *She is dressed to go out and carries a carrier with wheelie bin cover in it.*)
VERA	Are you ready?
MAVIS	Why, what time is it?
VERA	Half past one.
MAVIS	Bloody hell it's not, is it? I got all wrapped up in t' greenhouse. It's half past one, Stan, we're gonna have to get off!
VERA	You're alright for ten minutes . . .
MAVIS	Well I'm ready; I've just to find my script.

(MAVIS *picks up the tomatoes from the table.*)

VERA	They look good; Doug likes a tomato.
MAVIS	You can have some, we've plenty, haven't we, Stan?
STAN	We've not that many.
MAVIS	'Course we have, I'll put you some in a bag later on.
VERA	Well here . . . I've got sommat for you.
MAVIS	What's this, then?
VERA	Doug's sent it down for you.
STAN	What is it?
VERA	It's a flowered wheelie bin cover.
MAVIS	Oh bloody hell!
VERA	It's to help your bin blend in with t' garden.
MAVIS	That's a good idea, isn't it?
STAN	Just what we wanted.
VERA	It was a pack of two; they'd dropped right down to six quid. I tell you sommat; that Bid TV, I'm on it now!
MAVIS	Six quid?
VERA	It came with some secateurs and a dibber but I thought you'd already have one of them.
STAN	Ar, I've a couple of dibbers.
VERA	Dib, dib, dib, dob, dob, dob!

MAVIS	Tell Doug thanks, for that. I'll just get my stuff . . .
	(MAVIS *makes to exit, but* VERA *stops her.*)
VERA	How long do you think this read-through's gonna take?
MAVIS	With bloody Richard in t' main part, God knows . . . I mean to be honest I'm not that keen on *La Cage Aux Folles*.
VERA	Well don't worry because Doug thinks he can get us feathers in bulk on "QVC Craft Day Special".
MAVIS	I'd better get a move on; come in, Stan, and change your shirt!
	(MAVIS *exits into the house.*)
STAN	I need to put another can on here!
	(VERA *admires the display of flowers.*)
VERA	Stayed nice, hasn't it?
STAN	It will if you look after it. It'll go on until October if you dead head and feed it, Vera!
VERA	I can't believe that we didn't chuffin' win sommat.
STAN	The same woman won that won last year, didn't she? Still, it's brought sommat to my pond! I've just put a light in t' lighthouse. Looks rate good at night.
	(MAVIS *reappears. She has smartened herself up with a scarf and carries a handbag and casual briefcase.*)
MAVIS	For God's sake, Stan, we're gonna be late! Come on!

STAN	I'm not coming.
MAVIS	What?
STAN	I'm not going!
MAVIS	Why not?
STAN	Because I'm not!
MAVIS	After all we've said?
STAN	What's it about this new show, then?
MAVIS	*La Cage aux Folles*?
VERA	Well its not one for you, Stan!
	(VERA *exits through gate.*)
STAN	That's bloody relief, then.
	(*A beat.*)
MAVIS	We're going, then.
STAN	See you, then.
	(*A beat.*)
MAVIS	Bloody hell!
STAN	What's up now?
	(*A beat.*)
MAVIS	I give up!
STAN	No you don't.
MAVIS	Yes I do, Stan!
STAN	You'd've given up a long time ago if you thought like that.

	(*A beat.*)
MAVIS	I have done, Stanley. Believe me!
	(*Silence.* MAVIS *exits.* STAN *watches them go. He takes a moment to look around the garden. After a while he makes his way to the shed. He opens the door. We hear some drilling from inside. As he does this,* RIO *enters the garden from the downstage entrance. She sits at the patio table and eats some tomatoes.* STAN *comes from the shed with a dog kennel.*)
RIO	That's a good 'un!
STAN	It's a big 'un is this! I reckon this'll go for thirty quid, easy!
RIO	Well I've got seven orders so far, so . . .
STAN	If you get fifteen it'll pay for me and Mavis to go and see our Joanne. And not a bloody word, you. She knows nowt about it! Hey, if you come in here I'll show you how to make one.
RIO	No, you're right, I'll just sit here. I love it on your patio.
STAN	I used to show our Joanne how to make stuff. For a lawyer, she's a dab hand with a hammer.
	(*FX: Dog barking starts.*)
RIO	Oh here we go! Gonzo! Shuttit!
STAN	Thank God for that bloody dog!
	(*Music plays: "I Am What I Am" from "La Cage aux Folles". Music swells, and they admire the dog kenel. Music swells further as they laugh.*)
	(*Lights. Curtain.*)